Gypsy Jem Mace

First published in Great Britain in 2008 by

André Deutsch
An imprint of the
Carlton Publishing Group
20 Mortimer Street
London W1T 3JW

A CIP catalogue for this book is available from the British Library.

ISBN 978-0-233-00225-5

Typeset by e-type, Liverpool
Printed and bound in the UK.

The publishers would like to thank the following sources for their kind permission to reproduce the pictures in this book:

Plate 1: (top) Simon Knott/norfolkchurches.co.uk, (bottom): Private Collection;
Plate 2: Private Collection; Plate 3: Private Collection; Plate 4: Mary Evans
Picture Library; Plate 5: Antiquities of the Prize Ring; Plate 6: (top left) Private
Collection, (top right): Hulton Archive/Getty Images, (bottom left): ©Tavin/
Everett Collection/Rex Features, (bottom right): Bob Thomas/Popperfoto/Getty
Images; Plate 7 (top): John J. Bates/City of Kenner, (bottom left): Bob Thomas/
Popperfoto/Getty Images, (bottom right): AP/PA Photos; Plate 8 (top left):
Antiquities of the Prize Ring, (top right): PA Photos, (bottom left):
Dave Wood/Liverpool Pictorial, (bottom right): Private Collection.

Every effort has been made to acknowledge correctly and contact the
source and/or copyright holder of each picture. Andre Deutsch Limited
apologises for any unintentional errors or omissions, which will be
corrected in future editions of this book.

Gypsy Jem Mace

Jeremy Poolman

André Deutsch

Acknowledgements

I would like to thank the following, without whom the book you are holding would not exist:

Tim Bates at Pollinger, whose guidance and enthusiasm always make me want to do my best; Penny Phillips, who took the project on and saw it through its early stages; Vince Piffero, a good friend and fellow Norwich supporter, without whom *Gypsy Jem Mace* could not have been written; Gareth Jones, my editor at Deutsch, for his good humour, tolerance and attention to detail; Ben Laver, an immensely talented young man, for his support and gentle bullying; and Bob Lister, of course, for being my brother. Finally, I'd like to thank Sonia, my fiancée, Meg, Charlie, and my beautiful boy Joel for putting up with me and providing a reason for the whole endeavour.

For my father, at last

PROLOGUE

—✦—

The Past and the Future

ON THE DAY that my son turned three I discovered my father was dying. My sister called me with the news. My father and I had not spoken for two years. For me he was already as good as dead.

'Will you go?' she said. 'There's something he wants to give you.'

I said *no* but even then I knew that something craven inside me would, in the end, make me go.

And so I did.

I didn't know what to wear. It was like going on a date and I needed to make the right impression. Too smart and he'd be able to tell himself that what had happened wasn't *that* bad; too shabby and he'd think that I couldn't cope. And so, in the end, I settled on something unremarkable – neither one thing nor the other.

Also I had to decide whether to tell my wife I was planning to go. Ordinarily in those days we hardly spoke. Over the years I'd successfully infected her with my hatred and I feared that my seeing him now would seem to her like a betrayal. Mutual disregard of my father had brought us closer together – close enough to change our minds about not having a child.

On the train I tried to imagine what he'd look like – how the sudden failure of his heart to beat with any regularity might have altered his appearance. The last time I'd seen him he'd looked old but not sick. The last time I'd seen him he'd been planning a trip to Italy.

The hospital smelled of sickness and decay. The lift was rickety. I made my way sullenly to the ward.

'Your *father*?' The nurse's surprise told me that he'd not mentioned having a son. This buoyed up my flagging sense of injustice.

I spotted him at once when I entered the ward. He was as grey as

Lenin's death mask, his features half-familiar, like those of a waxwork dummy. It seemed quite impossible to me that I had come from him.

In a while the nurse re-appeared. She fiddled with the monitor and then she was gone. From the hall came the clattering sound of a tea trolley.

I sat by his bed for an hour. He didn't wake. I turned the pages of a newspaper. I looked out at the traffic.

There's something he wants to give you.

It was the kind of box-file he'd always used. As a child they'd been as familiar to me as the smell of his aftershave. Although I didn't know it then, what I found inside would change my life forever.

That night, driven by the need to confess, I told my wife where I'd been and what I'd found. I expected anger but received comfort. *The past and the future*, she said. Then we lay together, silent in the darkness listening to the sleeping sounds of our son.

PART ONE

What Kind of a Man

1

WHY THEY CAME to this bleak, windswept land no-one really knows. The passage of three centuries and the traveller's natural mistrust of the census have seen to that. And anyway, perhaps they didn't come here at all; perhaps they just *stopped* here. Perhaps the flatness of the land and the promise of good farming were enough to make them say *here we are and here we stay*. Or perhaps they were just simply too weary to go on. Whatever the reason, what we *do* know is that they – Jem's gypsy forebears – unhitched their ragged horses in this place and set down for good what little they'd brought with them.

They'd come all the way from the harsh, inhospitable mountains of eastern Europe, escaping the kind of bitter wind that freezes your fingers and stiffens the flesh of your face into a mask, at last fleeing the terrible hatred of their kind and fetching up after long months of travel in this tiny part of rural East Anglia.

——◆——

'Can I help you?'

'I was just looking at the stones,' I said.

It was there – *here* – that they chose to make a home for themselves, and for their children, and for their children's children too, and so on and so on, until the last of them was gone and is now barely a memory.

'Are you a relative?'

Yes, I said – but distant – and I told him my name.

The man nodded. 'I believe I knew your father,' he said.

'I know.'

He smiled. 'But that was a long time ago.' The smile drifted off. 'Is he well, your father?'

'He's in hospital.'

'Oh dear.'

We stood for a while in silence. A hand found my shoulder. 'A fine fellow your father. A real family man as I remember. Very interested in the ancestors.' He sighed. 'Of course they're mostly forgotten now.'

'That's why I'm here,' I said.

'To remember?'

And so it was – a foolish attempt to recover something of those lost memories – that had me heading up that slow Norfolk hill early last Spring toward a roofless church a mile from the village of Beeston, there to standing in the wind-battered, weed-strangled graveyard before an old marker.

Jem Mace

Champion of the World

Stolen, lost and then forgotten for so many years, the stone was apparently returned in 1976, having been discovered by chance buried deep under a mound of rubble in a Norwich builder's yard. After sixty years' weather its inscription now is battered and difficult to read, its surface rough and cratered like that of the moon. Carved in the shape of a cross it stands beside the gravestone of William Mace – Jem's father – and though I'd like to think of the two of them – father and son – lying together again side by side in the warm earth, they're not. The bones of the father are there but not those of the son. They lie four hundred miles to the north in a pauper's grave, buried in the shadow of Liverpool Football Club, from where, were Jem still able to, on match days he'd hear the crowds chanting like those that had chanted for him a century ago when he was in his pomp and was – for a while – one of the most famous men in the world.

'People say he was a great man.'

'Yes,' I said. 'I suppose he was.'

But he cannot hear those crowds and hardly a soul now knows his name. 'Jem who?' people say. 'Who was *he*?' Well as with any man, *who* takes time. It's surely better to ask first *what* he was, for he was no less than the last Bare-knuckle Heavyweight Boxing Champion of the World. As for *who*, well, to know that you have to know his story. To know that you must travel, as he did, several times around the world from New York to New Zealand; to know that you must walk the streets of Victorian London in the company of Charles Dickens and sit with the young Wyatt Earp playing fiddle in a Kansas City bar. You must stand and fight for forty-three rounds and then, when you're through, pick up your violin and play.

The man whom I later came to know as the Reverend Jonathan Boston bent down and touched Jem's stone like he might the head of a small child.

'Do you know what he was like?' he said. 'I mean what kind of a man?'

I shook my head. We stood a while longer in silence gazing down at the markers of father and son. *What kind of a man*. How difficult is that to know? How do you really get to know a man, to know what's inside him? I supposed then and believe now that all you can do is to walk in his footsteps and listen hard: to follow, in Jem's case, his steep rise and his even steeper fall.

'So what will you do now?'

'Make a start I suppose.'

'A start?'

'Where *he* started. Down there.'

Squinting in the early April sun we looked out and down the yellow hill. The village of Beeston was huddled low and brown. I looked at my watch. It was nearly noon.

—◦—

At precisely twelve noon on a fine April day in the year of 1831, Richard Nockolds climbed the scaffold that had been built especially for him in the ancient and genteel grounds of Norwich Castle. As he stood there in the mild sunshine, considering 'with a sharp and defiant eye' the fine wooden structure and the noose that would soon bring his wild and bitter life to an end, he didn't know – nor, in all likelihood, would he have cared – that at that very moment, only thirty miles north-east in the tiny village of Beeston, a young woman was in the final agonies of labour and would soon give birth to a tiny baby son. Nor did he know, as the hangman pulled the lever that released the trap-door, and those present heard the snap of a neck being broken and a death being judiciously delivered, that the baby boy, squalling with new life in the upstairs room of a labourer's cottage would, when older, speak his name to no lesser a person than Queen Victoria herself.

——•◆•——

'Richard Nockolds, ma'am—'

'*Who*, sir?' said the Queen.

On hearing the criminal's name Her Majesty (whose memory for such things was famously extraordinary) turned upon Jem 'the sharpest and beadiest of eyes'. That man, she said coldly, an echo of her German forebears still evident in her voice, had in her recollection been nothing but an incendiarist and an enemy of society.

All of which was essentially true. He had been, by any standard, a scoundrel, and it was certainly true that he'd lit up the vast Norfolk skies on more than a dozen occasions with reckless blazes that had cost several lives and terrified Earl Grey's Tory government with the threat of revolution. He had, however, had the awful fate of the common man in his mind – men like Jem's father William, who had walked barefoot all the way one Easter from Beeston to Norwich in search of a blacksmith's work, his belly sharp with hunger and his feet bruised and bloody from the long stony road. They were times when Richard Nockolds and others like him were the working man's only shield – long years when, after the theft of common land through enforced enclosure, the common man had been sentenced to a life of penury and servitude, or one spent incarcerated in the prison of the workhouse.

'Are you intending to speak, sir?'

'Yes, ma'am,' said Jem. And he did. He told her about his life – how his, in the same way as everyone else's, had begun long before he was born; how it had started centuries ago and thousands of miles away; how his father's journey on that long stony road from Beeston to Norwich had set a path for him that had led all the way around the world and back and had brought him here to the castle at Windsor on such a cold Winter's day.

'One is scarcely cold,' said the Queen. Her face though seemed to give the lie to this. It was sickly pale, especially so against the black of her mourning clothes. She looked old too, and exhausted – newly widowed but already wearied by the burden of loss.

How Jem's audience with the Queen ended we don't know. What we *do* know however is that in the days that followed, Jem returned for the first time in many years to Beeston – to the cottage in which he was born, to The Ploughshare Inn, to the old Cutter barn where as a young man he'd fought his first fights and where, in the exultation of victory and the agony of defeat, he'd discovered the strength, determination and willingness to suffer that would one day bring him such wealth and fame.

Indeed, if you look hard enough, you can almost see him there in the small yard behind the inn, a big man in his forties, his name known as well in New York and Sydney as it is in London, dropping to his haunches and laying his palms on the hard, cold earth of his youth. His fingers are thick and gnarled, the legacy of so much physical punishment and the cocktail of whiskey and gunpowder with which his hands had been prepared before every fight throughout his life.

'I thought of my father,' he once said, 'and my brothers, and tried to hear again all the shouting and cries that had once filled that yard.' But of course, for Jem, such cries and shouting were by then long gone. All that was left were memories.

2

FOR TWO CENTURIES the traveller who began his journey in the tiny village of Beeston and wished to end it in the city of Norwich had to travel east and a little bit south, passing through Wending and Dereham and Hockering and Easton before the three-pronged spire of Norwich Cathedral rose in the distance, its walls of French lime-stone pale yellow in the light.

Today of course things are different. Today it's the A47 that delivers you to the heart of what was once the nation's second city in little over half an hour. Back in 1830, though a man with means could hire a pony and trap and 'feel all his bones all colliding' on the badly rutted roads, if you were a poor man – a humble blacksmith like William Mace – and you wanted to travel the thirty or so miles ,then you walked.

How long the journey took William Mace that Spring no-one really knows – four, maybe five days. What we do know is that, when he crossed the Wensum River at Hellesdon Bridge on the morning of Thursday 17th April, he was tired and hungry, and that he was excited too at the prospect of the Fair. As he passed by the Horse Barracks and the Blind Institute on Magdalen Street he could already hear the sounds of the fairground at Tombland, the hawkers with their stalls already up and eager, the victuallers with their drays and great barrels of beer. As he turned the corner and saw before him the slow gentle rise of Castle Hill, it must have seemed to him then that all that was fine in the world lay before him.

The plan was to meet Thomas Wighton at the Fair. Thomas Wighton was a friend and carpenter from Cromer on the north Norfolk coast whom, though they'd been friends for scarcely a year, William had chosen to be his best man. He was a tall man, Thomas

Wighton, and thin – the very opposite of the bridegroom to be. To see them together was to witness the variety that was the genius of God's design, and to hear them laughing (something they often seemed to do) was to hear in the man the presence of the boy who never leaves him.

For William, aside from the general excitement of the Fair, his visit had one particular purpose. With the aid of Thomas Wighton, his task was to find a special present for his bride – something that could only be found in such an exotic and faraway place as Norwich.

The year of 1830 was the year of riots – of barns set to burn, regardless of the cries of the beasts trapped inside. It was the year too when the workhouse at Swaffham was burnt to the ground and those wretches caught sleeping were stripped by the flames of their flesh and then their lives. It was the year when the French working classes were once again rising up against their masters while, across the Channel, their cousins were setting the countryside alight. Haystacks roared ablaze in the darkness and smoky mornings revealed the wreckage of machines, whose grinding and threshing would deprive a man of his livelihood and consign his children to the workhouse or the arms of God and his scant and careless mercy. It was the year of Richard Nockolds and the landowners' fear of shadows.

'They say he'll be hanged if he's caught.'
'They'll not catch him.'
'Who'll be hanged?'
'Nockolds. They say they'll make an example.'
'An example?'
'Hang him by his neck until he's dead.'

It was all the talk that Easter at the Fair – in the ale tents and amongst all the merchants selling wool and corn, and boots from France – and there was even talk that Nockolds himself had been seen walking with the cross on its journey from the Chapel to the Sepulchre, while others were sure he'd been standing on the battlements of the Norman cathedral, a ghoulish smile on his face and blood on his hands.

For Thomas Wighton, more so than William, Richard Nockolds was a hero, a man whose ends justified all means. For him there could be no censure for a man who wished to free his fellow man however that freedom was achieved. If cattle were burnt to death and property destroyed then so be it. All that mattered was that the scourge of poverty and the grotesque imbalance of wealth be ended.

Not so William Mace. He was a quieter man, and less given to the theoretical; he had heard the howling of the burning beasts and could hear nothing beyond it. He was a man with a gentleness that some mistook for cowardice. His were a father's qualities of stoicism and forbearance close to the point of coldness, characteristics he would pass on to his sons – one of them in particular.

But that was all to come. That year at the Fair, while the talk was all of Nockolds and what would become of him, the two friends drank their dark ale and tested their strength with the hammer and bell, and watched the bare-knuckle bouts and the dog-fights in the square wooden pen that stood in the shadow of the Cathedral's ancient walls. And when night fell they laid down in their blankets on the banks of the Wensum River and watched the stars congregate in the faraway heavens.

The Chantilly lace that William bought for his bride all those years ago at the Norwich Easter Fair was given to her in due course.

But it was a journey that didn't end there. The lace was passed on, down through the generations, and was given by my father to my mother on the day of their wedding in 1956. On that day, while in the sunroom, as the radiogram (a wedding present from my maternal grandfather, who had once taken tea with Heinrich Himmler) spun out the new and thrilling voice of Elvis Presley, my mother stood in the garden beneath a bower of Albertine roses. One hand gently rested on the shoulder of her new husband, while the fingers of the other caressed the delicate loops and curls of a small square of now ancient French lace.

———

My father turns in his sleep in his hospital bed.

'I'm so lucky,' he whispers.

'Lucky?' I say.

'I do. Do you?'

My father's words are barely a whisper. I lean forward. 'I don't know what you're saying.' I turn away. 'I don't know what he's saying.'

The nurse lifts the chart and considers it.

'Is he often like this?'

'Oh, often,' she says, and then she is gone. I sit back. There is nothing to do but go on.

The child was born at noon on 8ᵗʰ April 1831. Any record of his birth weight or details of the delivery were either lost a long time ago or, as is the case with much of the information pertaining to the children of the rural poor, simply went unrecorded at the time and was then forgotten. What we can say, however, is that James Mace, son of William and Ann Mace (nee Rudd) was one of four brothers brought into the world in the upstairs room of a tiny labourer's cottage on the Wyndham Estate, across the road from what is still The Ploughshare Inn in the tiny rural hamlet of Beeston, Norfolk.

From the start the young James Mace was special. Or perhaps he was just different, *special* implying some prescience of what was to come. And no-one around him could have guessed that. When they could scarcely imagine what lay beyond the next hill, how could they possibly picture New York? When the spire of St Mary the Virgin at Beeston was the grandest thing they'd ever seen, how could they ever imagine the fjords of New Zealand or the blue sparkling waters of San Francisco Bay? Such a thing was impossible. You lived and died in the narrow world into which you were born; to stray was heretical and foolish, like believing the world to be flat but still sailing to its edge and then over. It was unhealthy, a kind of madness. Everyone knew it and it would have seemed so too for Jem had it not been for something inside him that said *why not take a look?* It was this gypsy need for freedom that had him walking by the age of six months and this perhaps that had made him wander the dirt lanes and worry his parents so.

'He cannot be held,' his father said, and he was right – not even by the simple expedient of a bolt. He would drag a chair to the door, rifle the bolt, lift the latch and be gone. Sometimes he'd be missing for hours and a search-party would be raised, only to be disbanded – often well after dusk – when the call came up from a barn half a mile away or the corner of a field somewhere where Jem had lain down exhausted and fallen into a young boy's deep and dream-filled sleep.

'I didn't know where I was bound,' he dictated several decades later. 'I only knew it was out there. Pooley too sometimes. Whatever it was it was *over there*. Further than either of us could see.'

Pooley Mace was Jem's cousin and for most of their lives his best and closest friend. The son of Barney Mace, he was seldom not there, a step behind his older cousin, ready to run where Jem ran and ready to scuffle with the other village boys when Jem did. They would wander the countryside together, hiding and seeking and tumbling together in the dust of Summer or Winter's heavy mud. They would wrestle and fight, unaware of the strength they were gaining every day and how, even as young boys, they were taking their first steps on a long and brutal journey.

It was a journey everyone thought was pre-determined by a poor man's circumstances. It would end – all were certain – pretty much where it had begun. Jem was the son of a blacksmith and the grandson of a blacksmith and would therefore become a blacksmith himself. It was a destiny that only the foolish or deluded would reject. It was as iron-cast as the hooves they made – you have hands and a strong back and it's what you do. And it's what he *did* do – though from the very start he hated it. He hated the monotony. He hated the smithy and saw it as a prison. He wanted to be outside, running, discovering. But like his brothers he was born to it. Like his brothers he had no choice.

Whether or not what happened to his hand was the result of a deliberate act we don't know – and he never said. All we do know is that – deliberate or not – one day he struck his hand with a blacksmith's hammer so hard that it swelled to the size of a melon. Whether bones were broken, again we don't know. What we do know is that his days as a smithy were, around the age of twelve, at an end. His father shouted and struck him as many fathers do, but then the storm was over. The boy, he said, was clumsy and ungrateful. Let him look to himself for his living. Let him waste his life by wandering the lanes if that was his choice. Let him choose his own journey and live with the consequences.

3

DOCTOR HUSSEIN, A man whom I have never considered to exhibit the most holistic view of his profession, has lately taken to showing an interest in my father's work. Whether this interest is genuine I cannot say. I, unlike he, it seems, cannot look inside another man's head and come to understand what makes him tick. I, like most of us, unlike the good doctor, am condemned to scuttle around like a rat in the hinterland of history, hopelessly looking for clues.

'So your father's a boxer too,' he says, as if he's telling me something I don't already know but should. Then, having nodded with seemingly false interest at a picture of the old Cutter barn, he departs, leaving me at the bedside of a man who can now scarcely breathe (let alone box), to wait for someone to relieve my vigil.

Whether or not in the course of his research my father ever really visited the site of the old Cutter barn I have no way of knowing for sure. His language certainly implies that he did. 'Voices of the past,' he writes, 'seem to eddy around, undisturbed by the presence of a dozen or more hikers, each one of whom displays the repugnant earnestness of a lycra-bound cyclist.'

———•———

Voices of the past.

Ghosts.

A barn long-destroyed, replaced by a filling-station and gift shop.

'Was it here?' I say.

'Aye,' says the man with black and white dog. He speaks with such certainty that you'd think he remembered it.

'What happened?' I say.

'Fire,' he says.

I watch him walk away then head for the gift shop in search of some Jem Mace memorabilia.

According to local maps, the barn stood a mile or so north of Beeston on the road that led to Cromer and the north Norfolk coast. Every Saturday night a crowd would gather here to watch two men from the local village strip to the waist and square up to each other, then beat each other senseless. When one was left standing and the other bloodied and broken and unable to see, all would know just who was the bravest and the strongest, and who consequently would have the pick of the prettiest girls of the parish. It was brutal but the times were brutal. More babies died in child-birth than lived, and a man's life was so hard that he was old by forty and dead by forty-five.

And so every Saturday night a crowd would gather in the old Cutter barn to watch men they knew and some they didn't, fight with the terrible recklessness of those whose crimes of poverty have not been forgiven – those already condemned to die.

On one such night Jem Mace, who was by then ten years old, slipped out of his parents' cottage to meet Pooley beneath the oak tree that stood on the banks of the stream that ran slow and quiet behind The Ploughshare Inn. Without saying a word they started off across the fields, all the time heading for the old Cutter barn.

Despite the season, by eight o'clock the light was already failing, the barn just a looming shape in the dusk. Pooley slowed as they approached, aware of the consequences of discovery.

'Do you think we should?' he said. He was the younger of the two and could already feel the harshness of his father's beating. But Jem kept on walking; for him the call of what lay ahead was far stronger than the fear of what lay behind. Careful of his footing he moved slowly along the side of the barn, Pooley behind him breathing hard. He paused and turned his head and put his eye to the gap between the barn's wooden beams.

'What's it like?' said Pooley. He could hear muffled voices inside.

Just how many men were gathered inside the barn was impossible to say. Three dozen, perhaps, maybe more. Some Jem recognized, though most were from villages too far away for their faces to be familiar. Familiar or not, most had the same look of furtive excitement about them; they were grinning like boys who, though they know better, are still determined to do wrong. But some of them were more serious. These men were giving and receiving coins and making marks on pieces of paper, and sometimes scowling and jabbing with their fingers. They were obviously important men – men of whom the others seemed wary and even afraid.

'What do we do now?' whispered Pooley.

'Come with me,' said Jem.

Pooley followed his cousin around the side of the barn. Here Jem dropped to his knees and pulled up a broad plank of wood and in a second was gone. Pooley looked around then followed.

It was smoky in the barn and filling up with noise and sweat. Unseen in the deep shadows of the corner, Jem and Pooley climbed up the hay bales and settled themselves on the edge with a fine view looking down. Below them there were fifty or sixty men now milling about, pushing and shoving and laughing and cursing. Most of them were drinking and some of them were drunk. Pooley looked at Jem but Jem was looking down, his face lit up with dread and excitement.

There was a roped-off square in the centre of the barn, a rough-made stool in each of two opposite corners. As if in response to an unheard signal, two men started picking their way through the crowd, some slapping them on the back while others cheered or cursed. The two fighters dipped down below the ropes. To Jem they seemed huge – twice the size of other men and as noble as kings. He watched them pout and preen and stride around the ring with outrageous arrogance, each one of them both hero and villain.

The smart money it seemed was on the big man with the belly. For him the cheers were louder and the booing less committed. He had a snarl about him and arms thick with muscle. He was taller too by a foot at least and wore a belt of thick rope around the bloated waist of his long sacking pants.

'He's from Hockering,' said Pooley, but Jem wasn't listening. His eyes were on the smaller man who, though shorter and lighter, had about him – what with the pointy look of his face and narrow eyes, and the relative spareness of his frame – a kind of vicious, feral meanness, as if for all the raising of his arms and his joshing with the crowd he was there not just to win but to beat a man senseless and then beat him some more just to watch him squeal in pain.

For a moment, when the man in the top hat raised his arm, all was quiet. But then – with the fighters in their corners – as he dropped it and the two men advanced on each other, the howling and the cursing and the spitting returned ten-fold, until surely not a soul in the parish could have heard a dog barking or a man with a shotgun shoot a horse that's gone lame. The clamour rose like a tide that threatened to drown every living soul present, and when the big man threw the first punch but missed and swung himself nearly all the way around, the smaller man's supporters let forth such a torrent of abuse that even high above in the rafters Jem knew that before he'd even really started the big man was beaten but would have to go on until he knew it too. And when the big man flung another punch and this met with the same result as the first, he lost his balance and tripped, and went down, hitting the ground hard but not so hard that he couldn't raise himself up again, just in time for the other man to hit him square in the face and break his nose. Blood at once cascaded like a red tide from behind a broken dam, and taking a punch to the gut he folded, and, as he fell back against the rope, he turned his face upward, as if to the sky or to God, sending as he did so blood and sweat and tiny chips of bone spraying out across the crowd, who howled and bayed for more. And there *was* more, for the big man wasn't beaten yet, and he dragged himself up on to his feet, and, for a moment in his mind's eye, Jem *was* that man and he could feel what *he* was feeling, and it was wonderful and terrible, and from somewhere inside him he found the strength to raise his arms as the other man battered him, and he felt the *crack* of another rib gone, and the blood in his mouth was salty like the sea, and like the sea something made his aching body go forward on and on, as wave after wave of bloody punches turned his head and split his ear, and he tried to shake the sweat and the blood from his eyes so he could see. But all he could see was the other man bleeding too, and how his teeth were just stumps, all yellow and jagged, and then there was cheering even louder and arms around him, but the pain was too bad now and too *everywhere* to matter, and when they raised him up and called him *Champion*, all he could think was *please let this never end*. But it was already ending and when the barn at last was empty, and the night was coming on and it was getting colder, with it came the knowledge that even a Champion is a solitary man...

When the morning came and it was damp and misty and he was lying where he'd slept in the old Cutter barn, he knew that from now on no-one would ever matter, and nothing – not family, not fear, not pain unto death – would ever get in his way until he, Jem Mace, was Champion of the Whole Wide World.

———

'Who?' says the woman in the gift shop.

I tell her again, this time attaching a short biography.

She shrugs then brightens. She withdraws a box from beneath the counter. She pulls back the flaps. I peer inside. The box is full of last year's calendars. She pulls one out and turns to February.

A Boxer dog, all eyes and teeth, and beneath it: *Treat your dog like a human and he'll treat you like a dog.*

'Thank you,' I say.

4

HE WAS AN absent father, always on the road, and, even when he was home, there always seemed to be endless unavoidable calls on his time.

I was wild and ashamed.

Any boy dismissed by his father as useless and ungrateful is likely to be a boy with something to prove – especially when the one to whom he looks for validation is never there.

And all I wanted was approval.

Which never came.

Instead the young man took to fighting, using what he'd seen in the old Cutter barn as a template, his fists held high and straight out before him, his feet planted firmly on the ground. By the age of fourteen he'd fought 'a score of battles' and though they were mostly defeats, what he learned from them was more valuable than victory's shallow lesson. He learned that it's not the getting knocked down that counts but the getting up again, and that strength and will are useless without belief.

They got me and I swore I'd get them.

They were the Stroud boys, chimney-sweeps the lot of them, all seven of them bigger and older than Jem.

And I did. Every one of them.

He picked them off one by one with an ease that surprised even himself, sending each one sprawling into the dirt until there was just one of them left.

James Stroud was the toughest of the lot. He had two years on Jem and a history of thuggery that made many in the village turn away when he came swaggering by. That he'd been mixed up in the riots (there were rumours around that he'd killed a man by slicing his belly from one side to the other with a butcher's cleaver), surprised not a soul in the least.

The fight was arranged for early one Sunday morning in the Cutter barn. The two of them would bring a man in support. For Jem that man was Pooley; for James Stroud, his brother (also James), who was still nursing a badly-broken arm.

The fight was over inside a minute. For all his size and strength James Stroud went down like his brothers and like his brothers failed to get up. Thus was the Stroud spell broken and Jem – for a few days at least – was a hero to the town's other boys. They were small beginnings, but beginnings nonetheless, for while, away in America a President died and the great gold rush began, Jem Mace the fighter was already starting to make his own history.

But local fame withers and even in a tiny village like Beeston time moves on. Soon, despite his famous victories, the hero became just another young man again with a young man's absent prospects. He'd proved he could fight – but so what? There had to be more. He had to *do* something.

Mr Fox, an acquaintance of Jem's father William, was a cabinet-maker in search of an apprentice. This, for a father with such a useless and ungrateful boy, was a chance too good to miss – especially so, as Mr Fox was Mr Fox of Wells-next-the-Sea, and Wells-next-the-Sea was far away, up on the north Norfolk coast.

The young man cried when the day came to leave – his mother too. His father said nothing; after a brief unspoken acknowledgement that the day would bring changes he returned to his work, leaving mother and son alone. She helped Jem gather his things, hardly daring to consider what might lie ahead. He'd a bundle of clean clothes tied up in a large red handkerchief and fixed to the end of a stick; fixed to the end of another, wrapped in blue cotton, was a meal of boiled bacon and dumplings. This she'd prepared for him in the early hours, having been quite unable to sleep. Lastly, wrapped in green baize, was Jem's old fiddle. The sticks he settled one on each of his shoulders; the fiddle he slipped under his arm.

All but the Stroud boys turned out to watch him go. They slapped his back and cheered and wished him luck as his boots raised pale dust from the dry summer road. In the smithy his father worked on.

CHAPTER FOUR

On the road Jem gradually left the village and his family behind him. He settled his walking into an easy rhythm and fixed his eyes on the distant horizon. He had a very long way to go.

—◆—

'How do you tell the difference between a fiddler and a dog?'

'Oh I know this one.'

'You do?'

But of course he doesn't. Now, if I'd have said, 'Doctor, I have yellow teeth, what should I do?', he would no doubt have told me to wear a brown tie. But I didn't and so he doesn't. Instead he just stands there checking my father's pulse and looking like he's something to say but isn't quite sure how to say it. He carefully lays down my father's hand. He cocks his head like a bird. He's frowning.

'Your father,' he says, then pauses.

'What about him?'

'You were close, were you?'

'Why?'

'Weren't you?'

'Why do you ask?'

'Oh, no reason.'

'There's always a reason.'

'Well, it was just something your mother said.'

'I doubt that.'

'Excuse me?'

And wouldn't you know it, just at the moment when it's all getting interesting his beeper beeps and he's called away.

'See ya,' I say, glad really to see the back of him.

—◆—

He made it in three days, the thirty-odd mile trip north from Beeston to Wells-next-the-Sea, passing through Mileham and Oxwick and on to Fakenham where he spent his first ever night away from home. Here he slept in a barn sharing the accommodation with two dozen cows thought to have Wooden Tongue Disease, a mostly fatal condition. The cows lowed so plaintively all night that by morning Jem found it hard to rise. But rise he did, gather his things and move on. He had ten miles to go.

Though today the Shrine of Our Lady of Walsingham has been rebuilt and expanded to include a guest house and a gift shop, when Jem was passing through it was no more than a ruin. It was still, however, a popular place of pilgrimage, and Jem, as with so many others before and since, stood amongst the tumbled stone and tried to take from the place what there was to be had. What this was he didn't say. Perhaps it was some kind of reassurance about the future or perhaps just a quiet place to sit and rest. Whether he asked for the shrine's blessing on his endeavours no-one will ever know. All we can say is if he *did* ask and the blessing was granted then it worked for a while but not forever – for the truly blessed surely don't end up where he did. The blessed, surely, after a long and happy life, die peaceful and content in their own clean-sheeted beds. Furthermore, the lives of the blessed are surely never in the hands of a cabinet-maker named Mr Fox, for whom cabinet-making was the least of it, the *most* of it being drink and women and sailors, and half of the smugglers and wreckers, whose trade was conducted after dark in the coves and rocky inlets of the north Norfolk coast.

5

MY MOTHER DIED in agony, tied to a wicker chair for her own protection, wracked with such pain in her last days that the morphine barely touched it. It would have been easier for us all had she spent those last days in hospital, but she insisted on coming home.

Three things in particular stick in my mind about the day she died. Firstly how, in an act of monumental insensitivity, the paramedic who pronounced her dead insisted that if I wanted her eyes closed then I'd have to do it myself; secondly that, on hearing of his wife's passing, my father's first words to my sister and I were *You'll have to look after me now*; and thirdly that she died on the same day of the year as Jem's mother, Ann. This last thing I only discovered many years later and, while it no doubt carries no more significance than coincidence is apt to, it is something that I cannot quite just file under *Fact* and forget.

For his part Jem never knew the exact moment of his mother's death – only, later, that she passed away one night while he was at work in The Green Dragon public house, his fiddle in his hand and his gypsy eyes smarting from the sweat and heat of the basement and its swirling acrid smoke. It was a night in fact like any other.

For the good Christian people of Wells-next-the-Sea, The Green Dragon was the place to which the weak, the unfortunate and the downright wicked finally sank when their lowest point had been reached and there was no more sinking to be done. Only the sea, people said, could drag a man deeper into depths less wholesome and further from the blessed light of God – depths from which a soul was certain never to return.

The proprietor, Mr Fox (a man whose Christian name is as lost now as a barnacled piece of driftwood bourne out on the tides), was a man of several parts. While it's true that he *did* provide sustenance and shelter to some of the wickedest men in that part of the county, and that he didn't object (or so it is said) to earning a few bob from their shady misdeeds, it is *also* true to say that he was a man who could allow himself to be quite transported by the sight of a beautiful woman or, indeed, a slow sweet lament played on an old beaten-up fiddle.

That his first experience of Jem wasn't something seen but heard has a sweet resonance about it. It tells us that both men – the illiterate, rough-mannered labourer and the sharp-featured, sneaky-eyed landlord – were men with more sugar in their bitter tea than either would care to admit. Even in a place as brutal as the Dragon's backyard (a place more used to cursing and sickness come from drink and the whisper like a knife's blade of deals struck in shadows), something as delicate as music could survive.

The young man was strongly built with a working-man's roughness. He was sitting on an upturned bucket, his handsome face fixed in a look both of ease and concentration, a fiddle gripped tightly beneath his chin, his bow moving slowly, this way and that, with elegance and precision, fiddle and bow making music so sweet and melancholic that it moved Mr Fox as he'd scarcely been moved in six decades. He set his stubby hands on his hips and gave himself up to listening. Jem went through his entire repertoire, finishing with an improvised piece he called his 'Cuckoo Solo', in which he 'mimicked all the birds of the air, the cuckoo's note being made to sound in and over at intervals'.

When Jem had finished playing the two men exchanged names and shook hands. Mr Fox knew at once, of course, that a man with the talent and looks of this newcomer would be wasted in a workshop; such a man, he was certain, would find life much more agreeable making music for his punters in the pub's dingy basement – not to mention at the same time adding a certain touch of class to proceedings.

'So tell me young man,' he said, his best smile revealing a set of short, pointed teeth, 'have you ever made money with that fiddle of yours?'

'Here and there,' said Jem.

'For pennies?'

Jem hesitated.

'Not shillings, then.'

'I thought it was cabinet-makers you were wanting,' he said.

Mr Fox shook his head. 'Oh it *is*,' he said. 'But any fool can do that. Look, are you hungry?'

'Well...'

'I could show you to your room right away, if you like. It has a very pleasant aspect. And then we could eat.'

'There's a room?'

'For a fiddle-player.'

'And a cabinet-maker?'

Mr Fox smiled slyly.

'My father sent me here to learn a trade.'

'So learn a trade,' he said. 'Learn to give people what they want.' He frowned. 'And by the way, how *is* the drunken old fool?'

And so it was that Jem's career as a cabinet-maker ended before it had begun, and a young man, for whom wickedness was only something preached against at St Mary's on a Sunday and wasn't truly real, stepped down into the world of Mr Fox and The Green Dragon's Club Room. Being a young man of little experience, he didn't know that such a world was one from which a person cannot hope to escape without some kind of stain on his soul or scar on his skin that will stay with him for life.

——◆——

'Is that all?'

'Isn't it enough?'

Today what was then The Green Dragon is now a thrift shop where everything on display costs a pound. Plastic bowls are a pound, as are boxes of detergent, dusters and novelty key-rings and a modest selection of books. Among the latter are crudely-printed abridged editions of *War and Peace*, the covers of which show a man in a pantomime uniform clinging onto a wildly rearing horse, the city of Moscow burning behind him.

'Would you like a box of Jaffa Cakes?'

'How much are they?'

The underfed girl behind the counter sighs. 'A pound,' she says. 'Everything's a pound.' She looks at me harshly: it's a joke she's heard a thousand times.

But I didn't mean it as a joke. I want to say *honestly, no, some-times I just don't think*, but her scowl stops me dead. I pay for the book and the box of Jaffa Cakes and slope out, embarrassed by what I said and what I didn't mean.

I sit on the jetty and count the beached fishing boats. The sea is grey and the sky too. I eat a few Jaffa Cakes then take out the book.

'Are you looking for a boat?'

I shake my head and watch the old man walk away. He is old – seventy, eighty maybe – and he walks with the roll of a sailor. In a moment he's out of sight. I go back to my book.

Towards the end of *War and Peace*, Tolstoy addresses the conflict between Freewill and what he calls the Law of Necessity – how the passage of time alters our perspective on the cause or causes of events. Close up, he says, an event is most likely to be seen as the result exclusively of Freewill; that is that the man who throws a punch, for example, was always entirely in command of that action. However, let enough time pass and that punch will come to be seen as the result of all that has gone before – that in effect its throwing was inevitable. In other words, we only ever really choose a path that has already been chosen for us by our history.

———

When Jem, thanks to his father, found his way to Mr Fox and his Club Room, he had no way of knowing that he was entering a world in which the exercise of man's freewill was circumscribed by both the thick and binding vine of the mid-century criminal underworld and the rather more sinister realm of the occult. Left to atrophy for a century or more, the practice of witchcraft had itself, since the slow awakening of the nation's industrial future, begun a revival, as if in response to some fundamental human need. Consequently, especially in the more rural areas of the country, where the benefits of the railway's creeping development were slowest to show themselves, the presence of witches became once again not uncommon and the practice of alchemy re-emerged.

Alchemy.

The search for a method of turning base metal into gold or an elixir to prolong life indefinitely.

No wonder then, in times so fraught with change and uncertainty, that the already disenfranchised should seek some redress through that which could not be fenced in or explained by the new 'science' or overrun by tracks of wood and steel. For some this meant a rebirth in Christ, for others something else altogether. For those who made their way down the twenty-three steps that gave access from The Green Dragon's courtyard to the Club Room – the smugglers, the pick-pockets, the sharp blades for hire, or those whose only crime was to live on the edges of villainy – it meant allegiance to another deity. This was neither man's ancient creation of some all-seeing God nor the modern 'God' of science but the fearsome and decidedly unholy practice of witchcraft.

At first Jem was unaware of what was going on around him. He just sat in the corner and played his fiddle, while the Club Room's patrons drank their ale and filled the air with smoke and talk. Now and then a scuffle would break out; when this happened, Jem would lay down his fiddle and, with the strength that youth and nature had so generously given him, separate the combatants and send them on their way.

It was only after a few months of being in Mr Fox's employment that Jem came to realize what so many of the Club Room's patrons had in common. Being unused even to the *usual* ways of the town, how was he to know what was usual and what was not?

One night, driven both by loneliness and curiosity Jem detoured from the route of his nightly walk. He had started towards a group of men who were standing on the quayside, but something made him stop in the shadows from where he observed the most curious sight. The men were surrounding a gaggle of what looked like chickens, each of which, being uncharacteristically quiet, must either have had its beak bound together or its tongue plucked out. Soon, after a deal of muttering, the chickens were thrown, one to a man, into the water where each one of them struggled briefly, then sank and died. The death of each chicken was greeted with a low mournful sound from the men and a general shaking of heads. Then they turned away in silence and walked back to The Green Dragon.

From his place in the shadows Jem recognized all but one of them as regulars of the Club Room. He held his breath as they passed by and, when they were gone, he made his way down the cobbles to the jetty. He peered into the murky water. There, lit by a three-quarter moon, he saw not what he expected to see but something quite different. What he saw looked for all the world like a corpse – a man, certainly, and tall – floating face down, his arms spread wide, as if he were testing the water for width or unsuccessfully attempting to fly.

'I watched him,' Jem said, several decades later, 'expecting him to turn or perhaps to start swimming. But neither thing did he, and I came to believe that the poor man was indeed gone from the world.'

The 'poor man' was Job Piggin, whose presence in the town had, for several months, gone mostly unnoticed. Those who had made his acquaintance described him as a man who spoke little and smiled even less. He was, they said, surely a man with a secret, though no-one seemed to know what it was. In a world of secrets one more didn't signify. And so they let him be, until he turned up one night in The Green Dragon's Club Room and laid his battered old bowler hat on the bar.

To some they were wizards. To others they were wisemen. Some knew them as witch-doctors, others as conjurers. However, it is known that, by the mid-nineteenth century, there were several thousand of them plying their trade in England's rural counties. They were the Cunning Men and Cunning Women, and whether or not they were genuine – whether they really possessed abilities sufficient to strip 'black' witches of their powers – depends largely now on the onlooker's inclination. Many, of course, were charlatans (for the fake always follow where the genuine make a profit), though whether or not Job Piggin was one is impossible to say. All that can be said for sure now is that those Green Dragon regulars, whom poverty and disaffection had turned towards witchcraft, believed him to be genuine and so considered him a mortal enemy.

He'd begun his adult life as an English tutor to the children of the gentry in Suffolk and northern Norfolk. When this proved to bring him little reward, either socially or financially, he set himself up as a medical man (despite having no suitable training whatsoever) specializing in the lifting of 'trances', the suffering from which had become very popular in the second and third decades of the century. In order to cash in on the deliciously energizing fear of witchcraft then prevalent among the monied classes, he went to London and took instruction from Mr John Spottiswoode, the famous mesmerist and occultist. On his return to East Anglia some months later he put what he'd learned into practice. Exactly how many trances and evil spirits he identified and banished can never be known – nor can we identify when the pursuit of profit gave way to the desire to give comfort to the suffering and root out the presence of the Devil in man for its own sake.

The body of Job Piggin was washed ashore twenty-five miles east along the coast at Sheringham, though not identified as such until John Spottiswoode came to hear of it and the long process that led to his eventual identification was set in motion.

Among the articles discovered in Job Piggin's room were a number of small glass bottles, some containing powders of different colours and others a clear liquid. There was also a small leather-bound book containing words written in a language that no-one could read. Many years later, Jem showed the book to a man in New Zealand who had studied classics under the great Oxford scholar Thomas Brooke. This man, a Dunedin gentleman farmer, translated the contents and announced not only that it was written in Latin, but also that it was a book of spells. Among those spells, aptly for a boxer, was one to be used by the weaker man against the stronger in a fist-fight. Whether Jem ever used it or not he didn't say. What he *did* say was that, once in the ring, a fighter should fight with 'every part of his being', and this is clearly what he did.

———

'But of course it was all just hocus-pocus—'

'How do you know?'

'Which, just because it's not real, doesn't mean it doesn't *work*. If you truly believe yourself blessed or cursed, and you believe it strongly enough then you are.'

'And that makes sense?'

'No. But who said it has to make sense? A person lives up to who they think they are.'

'Well, I think I'm a genius.'

Niall Johnson, Professor of History at the State University of

Maine shrugs. His face breaks into a smile. 'Could just be that you're hungry,' he says.

We walk three blocks and eat lunch at the counter in Riley's RibShack. On the wall is a series of boxing prints, of everyone from John L. Sullivan to Mike Tyson.

Niall taps his knife on the counter.

Rufus Riley dips his head down through the serving window. He's red-faced and jowly, a once-promising amateur fighter.

'My friend here says Mace was a witch. Says he won the title by casting a spell. What do *you* think?'

'What do *I* think?'

'Hey, I didn't say he *was*—'

'*I* think that's BS.'

'That's what I thought you'd think.'

'Then why did you ask me?'

'I needed your authority.'

'My *what*?'

'You being a fighter.'

'Was.'

'Are you saying you never did a little voodoo?'

'No, sir.'

'Then you're a lucky man, Rufus.'

'No, sir – that wasn't luck. I got a wife and a TV set.'

'So?'

'So they're both working. Now *that's* luck.'

'You're a man amongst men, Rufus.'

Rufus looks at me. 'So who are you anyway? What's a fighter like Mace to you?'

Something stops me telling him the great-great-grandfather thing. 'Just interested,' I say. I exchange a glance with Niall.

'Well, let me tell you,' says Rufus, 'what I know about witches.' He pauses.

'Go on,' says Niall.

Rufus Riley takes the dish-cloth from around his neck and wipes his hands like a priest in preparation for the Mass. 'Never,' he says nodding gravely, 'summon anything you can't banish.' He stands back, set his hands on his hips. 'What do you think about *that*?' he says.

'It's brilliant,' says Niall. 'Where'd you get it? Some old fighter tell you that?'

He shakes his head. 'The first wife's lawyer,' he says. Then he shrugs and turns away, while the cruel old jukebox clicks, as if cued, and out from behind its bright lights spins the high, plaintive voice of Miss Tammy Wynette.

Whether or not it was the curious death of Job Piggin, or perhaps Mr Fox's notoriously reluctant distribution of hard-earned wages, that caused him to leave the other-worldly embrace of The Green Dragon and its Club Room now matters little; all that matters is that one evening Jem picked up his fiddle along with the rest of his meagre possessions, and left Wells-next-the-Sea behind him, heading west along the coast. This time he had no destination in sight and only the sea and the vast star-filled sky for company.

He found work at Holcombe Hall sawing up tree-trunks that had fallen in the recent storm. It was hot for the time of year and the work hard, but he stuck it out and was paid a wage promptly when he was finished. The following day he spent lying in the dunes with his arms aching from the sawing, uncertain as to what he should do now. He was a young man in his prime but all he had was a fiddle and a bunch of old clothes on the end of a stick. He had nowhere to go and nowhere to stay and he was tired of it. He had no choices but one.

He arrived home just as the family was sitting down to eat. His mother rose and hugged him; his father, she said, was sleeping upstairs. His brothers gathered around him.

Hey, where've you been?

What's it like?

Is it as wild as they say?

Were there girls?

He answered their questions as best he could then made his way slowly upstairs.

Useless and ungrateful.

He stood like a mourner beside his father's bed and watched the old man breathing. His breath was coming slow and hard. He looked different now – his face sallow, the skin drawn tight across his skull.

He stirred, his lips opening as if he were planning to speak, then closed again. He turned to the wall and breathed on.

Jem lay awake that night listening to his brothers' snoring and the creaking of the house. All he could think was *I'm back where I started – back to the life of a child.* But though he was no longer a child, he was still so far away from the Champion he believed he would become.

Jem rose just before dawn. Carrying his stick and his fiddle, he crept through the house and lifted the latch as he'd done so many times in the past. He closed the door quietly behind him and started walking.

He wandered the lanes of East Anglia for eight months, playing for pennies on street corners and outside public houses. Sometimes on Sundays he'd stand at the door of a church and move his bow to the sound of 'Softly And Tenderly Jesus Is Calling' or 'Angels From the Realms Of Glory', and he'd smile politely when the coins struck the bottom of his tin. Sometimes, if he was lucky, he'd find himself a part of the pre-dinner entertainment in the home of some grand lady or gentleman; on such occasions he'd play 'The Gypsy' – scowling and looking thrillingly deceitful – so ensuring the best return on his efforts. Sometimes, besides the agreed fee, there'd be a meal below stairs and perhaps even a glass or two of warm beer. Often, though, there was nothing, and his bed was a hay-bale in a barn or the cobbles in the corner of an alley. Sometimes it must have seemed as if that was all there was for him. He couldn't go home again – but what else was there? Sometimes it was hard for him not to believe that the life he had now was the life he'd always have – that it was the best life he could expect.

But then, one fine September day, he took a walk to the Thetford Autumn Fair.

6

THAT AUTUMN OF 1849 ice stopped the flow of the Falls at Niagara and Frederic Chopin – wracked with consumption – died on the island of Majorca. Meanwhile, her Majesty the Queen declared the Great Hall of London's Euston station open and, thanks in part to the life and death of that scoundrel Richard Nockolds, the iniquitous Corn Laws – for so long no friend to the poor – were finally abolished.

But that was all in the *world* and Jem was not yet a part of it. For now *his* world was Thetford and the Fair, his feet and calves aching from so much walking and a debilitating hunger in his belly. *His* world then was just the Fair's jostling crowds and the smells, sweet and foul, and the barkers' voices raised in urgent supplication – *Step this way, ladies and gents, come see the unfortunate creature and judge for yourself if it's human* – all that and the grinning women of the street, whose faces were as raddled now as whatever was left of their souls. There was mutton spitting like the Devil over fires tended lazily by filthy, wide-eyed children; there was cheap ale and cheaper gin, and the stink all around of lives lived precariously on the edge of despair. For Jem, as he drifted through the sweating raucous crowds, it must have seemed like there was nothing and no-one on his side – as if whatever guides and enriches an honest man's life had surely abandoned him. Then, when at last he was standing on the Fair's furthest edge, free of the pushing and shoving of the crowd and he couldn't think what to do any more, what he *did* do was simply lay himself down in the cool evening air beneath the Autumn-stripped arms of an old English oak. He let his eyes close, aware that the dreams that had once seemed so close were dreams no longer, but memories of dreams.

All of which was to reckon without Mr Edward J. Balls, former bank clerk and failed jockey (he grew too large, he said, on a diet of puddings) – a man of such famously extensive life experience that some claimed he had once done a turn for the Queen at Astley's Amphitheatre in Lambeth, while others were convinced he'd been engaged to the third and prettiest daughter of the King of all the Belgians.

'So can you play that thing?'

'Who wants to know?'

Mr Edward J. Balls lifted his top hat and announced himself with all the gusto of a man for whom every new day is an unlooked-for bonus. He pointed to the fiddle. There would be, he said, a shilling in it – two if Jem could play something Irish.

'You don't sound Irish,' said Jem.

'No?' Mr Edward J. Balls gave a broad and gleaming smile. 'Well how's this for Irish? A duck walks into an Irish bar. The barman says, "Hey, your trousers are down."'

'What?' said Jem.

'Your trousers. *Down.*' Mr Edward J. Balls frowned hard. 'Do you not get it?'

Jem shook his head – the man was quite clearly mad. He stood up. 'Look...' he started, but when he turned and tried to walk away a hand on his shoulder bade him stop.

'So have you somewhere to stay?'

'Is it your business?'

The smile on the face of Mr Edward J. Balls returned. It was the smile, if ever there was one, of a gentleman rogue, who's really more gentleman than rogue. 'Shall we go?'

'Go where?'

'I've something to show you,' he said, spicing his words with all the mystery he could manage.

The Edward J. Balls and Sons Gentlemen's' Boxing Booth was located that year, as every year, at the very centre of the Fair. An unusual construction of wooden poles and canvas blinds, once you'd paid to get in you'd find yourself in the company of men of all stripes – swells with their tops hats and ivory canes, merchants and farm owners in waistcoats and leather boots, labourers and refugees from the workhouses and slums in whatever attire fate and circumstance had provided. There were women too – but mostly it was men. It was fighting they came for and blood that they wanted. The pain of others was the perfect leveller, knowing as it did no barriers of class and station. The Champion would batter away at any man brave or foolhardy enough to challenge him and, while on almost every occasion it was the challenger who left the ring, bones broken and feet first, he'd leave behind him the sound of money changing hands – most of which, in the case of The Edward J. Balls Gentlemen's Boxing Booth, would find its way into the pockets of a man who may or may not have once been engaged to the third and prettiest daughter of the King of all the Belgians, not to mention having supposedly once done a turn for the Queen.

Mr Edward J. Balls leaned in close. He had to shout to make himself heard above the din. 'So what do you think?'

'About what?'

'Would you try it?'

In the ring, the Champion – a muscle-heavy square-chested Irishman named O'Reardon – was dancing and grinning and stepping just out of reach as his opponent spent the last of his energy in a hopeless display of desperately flailing arms.

'Fighting, you mean?'

Following which the Champion, swinging his right fist in a long raking arc, sent the poor fellow clean out of the ring, where he lay in a bloody heap at the feet of the ghoulish braying spectators.

'Come with me.'

Jem felt the hand again on his elbow. The spruce little man led him from the ring through a heavy canvas flap and out into the milling crowd. 'Well?' he said.

'Well what?'

They were standing in an alleyway between two large canvas tents. Mr Edward J. Balls had a look of great seriousness on his face.

'What do you want?' said Jem.

Mr Edward J. Balls smiled. 'What I want,' he said, '*is*, young man, to buy you some supper.'

There was pork in thick gravy and apple laced with cinnamon. It filled his belly and the rich frothy ale made him sleepy. The little man before him held out his hand; Jem took it and shook it.

'Splendid. You'll not regret it.' He reached for his flask. 'Whiskey?' he said.

Jem shook his head.

Mr Edward J. Balls took a swig then wiped his mouth with the back of his hand. 'Tell me,' he said. 'Do you know why the Lord created whiskey?'

Jem felt his eyes start to close.

Mr Edward J. Balls took another swig, then screwed on the top. 'In order,' he said, replacing the flask in his pocket, 'to stop the boys from the Emerald Isle ruling the world.'

Almost nothing that people know about Mr Edward J. Balls is true. No record exists, for example, to show that he ever performed for the Queen, nor could he possibly have promised to marry the Belgian's King's daughter. And as for the claim that he'd plunged headlong inside a barrel down the Falls at Niagara, it is plainly false, as must be the accusation that he'd once been censured by *The Times* for having been detained one Christmas Eve at the top of the Old Kent Road on a charge of Behaviour Unbecoming to a Gentleman.

In fact all we *can* be sure of is that he was the son of Edmund Balls, a paperhanger, and that he was born at a house that gave onto the Moon And Stars Yard in Lambeth, south London. After that, until the appearance of the Edward J. Balls Gentlemen's Boxing Booth, in historical terms he ceases to exist. Only with Jem's appearance is his strange life resurrected.

With one exception. We *do* know he had a daughter called Ruthie and we know that Ruthie was not a girl unused to the attentions of men. She was by all accounts a striking young woman, who wasn't shy of indulging that attention. When she saw a man she liked the look of she set out to get him, almost always with success.

Unsurprisingly Jem was such a man. He was tall and athletic and lonesome for the home he'd abandoned. For Ruthie he was perfect and she wasted no time. She smiled at him shyly then turned her head away. With a gesture as casual as this is the future of a man so often decided.

'Is your sister here?' the doctor asks.

'No. Why?'

He smiles. 'When she is, it'd be useful to talk that's all.'

'About?'

'Just a catch-up.'

'I'll tell her.'

He turns away and is gone.

I look at my father. Breath bubbles in his chest. I look for assistance but the nurses' station's deserted. He lifts his arm and beckons me close. His breath is warm, corrupt. He whispers the first line of a childish limerick. *There once was a cowboy from Yuma.* What it has to do with anything now I don't know. All that was a thousand years ago now, the Rattlesnake Motel empty now except for the writing on the wall in room 27:

> *There once was a cowboy from Yuma,*
> *who told an elephant joke to a puma.*
> *His body now lies*
> *under hot desert skies,*
> *for the puma had no sense of humour.*

Haha.

He slips back and I wait for an hour for my sister to come. She doesn't appear. The shift on the ward changes. Buttons are pressed and charts consulted and, for a while, all appears busy, businesslike. But then the low hum of inaction returns and visiting comes to an end. At the station the nurse turns the pages of a magazine. She looks up. I want suddenly to tell her what he did but the look in her eyes says *no*.

'He's doing well,' she says. I thank her and go. I head for my car as the rain begins to fall.

The storm that comes that night pulls the gutter from the wall above the bathroom window and buckles the fence at the end of the garden. I try to sleep but I can't. Strange, bitter dreams assail me. In the morning, bleary-eyed, I find a hedgehog dead on the step outside the back door.

—•—

In later years, despite the withering effect of fame and fortune on the past, Jem would often talk with his cousin Pooley about Thetford and how it was the fight with O'Reardon that had really changed his life. That was the moment he first knew what he was really meant to do. Indeed, though the line from Thetford Forest to the bayous of New Orleans is anything but straight, it is for him at least unbroken. That fight and all that came with it was something he'd be trying to reproduce for the rest of his life, even when his strength was fading and the man across the ring was younger and fitter and hungrier.

But all that was to come. Then there was just O'Reardon and his broad Irish smile and his body, thick with muscle, heavy and sinewy like the muscle-bound physique of a bull.

'You ready?'

Jem could hardly hear the voice above the howling, baying crowd. He dipped beneath the rope, shot a last glance at his employer, then stood tall and advanced.

Almost at once the smart money (most of which had been placed on the Champion) looked less smart. With the first great swing of his fist O'Reardon was so wide of his target that he swung himself nearly all the way around, as, stoked with booze, the crowd cheered and booed. At the sight of the next swing, Jem stepped back, and the outcome was the same. This time O'Reardon was so disorientated that he stumbled and nearly fell – and would have done had he not leaned on Jem for support. Jem looked to his corner. Mr Edward J. Balls was nowhere in sight. The only faces he recognized were Ruthie's (she was smiling, teeth gritted, her fist before her face clenched and urging him on) and the face of Balls' cousin, a girl who never spoke. He pushed back, shoving the Champion off him. The Champion was already breathing hard, his face and his chest and his forearms wet with sweat. A minute was usually all it took him – just one swing and it was over.

But not this time.

This time as the sweat stung his eyes and made it difficult to see, he was surely aware, as the young man stepped forward, that something was over and something else just beginning, and that much more of this and he'd end up not a hero but a joke for just as long as people out there remembered him – which wouldn't, he knew, be so terribly long. And so the Champion came again. This time the young man stood his ground in the face of this last great swing. Far from stepping back, the one they were already calling *JemJemJem* stepped forward, blocking the punch with his forearm and answering with one of his own. The Champion staggered back, then briefly seemed to gather his balance again, before crumbling at the knees and falling with the thud of a great tree cut down after a thousand years or more of growing.

Jem was appalled and amazed by what he'd done, as if he didn't know what to do next. He looked around at the crowd – at their filthy twisted faces, at their yellow teeth, at the women with their ragged shawls, at the men with their long-forgotten dreams – and there was something awful and wonderful in it all. And when they dragged him from the ring and under the rope, and hoisted him up high and he was riding on their shoulders around and around, he knew there was no going back and raised his voice up, for he knew for certain that that glorious night would never end.

The morning when it came was misty, the ground beneath him churned-up and muddy. He pushed himself up. He was lying beneath a damp tarpaulin beside the boxing booth. All around him were the sounds of other tents coming down, of the Fair being packed up and preparing to move on. Wagons struggled for grip in the mud, and horses, sweating, their nostrils flaring, objected to such hard and heavy work. Overhead thick clouds moved slowly across the sky.

'So how are we this morning?'

'Cold,' said Jem.

Mr Edward J. Balls took out his flask. Jem declined.

'Where's everyone going?'

'Going? Peterborough. Are you coming?'

'What about O'Reardon?'

'Gone.'

'Gone where?'

Mr Edward J. Balls shrugged. 'Ireland do you think?' he said, then nodded. 'Yes, it'd be Ireland I say. That'd be my guess. Gone to see his sweet old grannie, so he has.'

A cry went up above the banging and cursing.

'So are you with us? It's ten shillings a week. You sleep where you can find a place. All meals provided.'

A thick-set, vicious-looking dog barreled past in the mud. Jem watched it until it disappeared behind Jack Wallace's Ale Tent.

'Well?'

Jem turned back. He raised himself up and put out his hand, and thus was the deal concluded.

7

THE RATTLESNAKE MOTEL stood then, and stands now, a mile out of Yuma on the road heading east. Find the Marine Corp Rifle Range and you've found it. At night, through the thin walls, you can hear the *pop-pop-pop* of rifles as the soldiers prepare for war in Iraq. *Just boys*, my father would call them, until the drink got hold of him and he'd call them something else. *Then* they were murderers and were headed straight for hell.

It was in Yuma, and specifically in room 27 of the Rattlesnake Motel, that my father first told me about Jem Mace and that he was my great-great-grandfather. I was thirty-nine years old and he'd never told me before. Why I didn't know. Now I do. Now with the *Notes* before me it's clear. He thought I would steal it if he told me. He thought I would write his book. Which now I suppose I am.

Now, years later, as I sit here with him, ignoring the gathering coolness of the room while attempting to decipher his spidery handwriting, I suppose I have become what I always dreaded I would.

A ghostwriter. Just the chronicler of other people's lives.

But to return to the *Notes*. As I turn the page, an unseen hand somewhere turns on the lights. Suddenly the world outside is dark. Suddenly it's night again.

———

They travelled all over East Anglia, part of a ragged train of wood and canvas whose company were the fire-eating gypsies and bejewelled fortune-tellers, the strongmen and the bearded ladies. Like some bizarre rag-tag army they scoured the county and sometimes beyond, scavenging and grafting, all the time thinking of the next town, the next meal, the next fool with money in his pocket.

For Jem, each new town meant new challengers – the pale clerks, all skin and bone, who fancied their brains over the Champion's brawn, the labourers and factory-workers whose brawn was a match but whose brains were not, the young gentlemen who discovered that good breeding is useless when it comes to a fist-fight, the drunks whose courage was entirely liquid and flowed away as quickly as their strength. They all came and all went, some retiring from the ring to avoid a beating, some leaving feet first as the consequence of one.

Besides providing a means of food and shelter, these months he spent with Mr Edward J. Balls and his Gentlemen's Boxing Booth gave Jem a kind of rudimentary education, without which he would scarcely have been able to survive in the prize-fighting world. An illiterate nineteen-year-old, who would never learn to read or write beyond the standard of a very young child, he did somehow develop an ability to read his opponents – to understand instinctively their weaknesses and strengths, and to know, therefore, how to beat them. And, just as importantly, he was offered the harshest lessons of the fighting world – that any sentimentality displayed is certainly a sham, that every career ends in some form of defeat, and that the slide of a fighter on his way down is steep and that no-one will be there to greet him at the bottom.

'Excuse me.'

With the night comes stillness and the glow of a lamp at the nurses' station. I look up from my reading.

'Are you a relative?'

'Yes,' I say. 'Are you?'

Against the black of his suit the man's collar is as white as an African's teeth. He smiles. 'How distressing,' he says, glancing at my father. He looks back. 'Are you—?'

'Am I what?'

'It's just I heard he had a son, and I was wondering—'

'He left,' I say.

'Oh.'

'Anything else?'

'Well, no...'

A moment passes. I look down at the *Notes*. The man pauses for a moment then turns away. I hunch over a little more.

He was nineteen years old.

I reach up, twist the lamp. A pool of yellow light settles on the page.

———•———

He was nineteen years old in the spring of 1850, and weighed between ten and eleven stone. He was fit and strong and had grown both to love and to fear the booth, just as a man who discovers in himself a gift for painting comes, over time, both to love and to fear the canvas. With every day he remained unbeaten, his reputation grew and so, in the hearts of many, did the hatred of this uppity gypsy. What right had such as man to proclaim himself 'Champion' and take the hard-earned money of *genuine* Englishmen? He was after all a foreigner. He might as well be a Frenchman. Here and there scribbled words – *gipsi scum, bastard mace* – began appearing on walls, and now and then there was hissing and long looks in the street. But he looked away. It was what his heritage had led him to expect.

Day after day and night after night he fought, from the north coast of Norfolk to the villages at the southern end of Essex that, even during his lifetime, would become part of the great metropolis of London connected to the city by trainlines and tarmacadam roads.

Opponents came at him in all shapes and sizes, some sober, others drunk on booze and bravado, all hopelessly ill-prepared and every one of them destined to wake the next morning with a bruised and battered body, and the determination never to do such a foolish thing again. *Oh I had him alright*, they'd say, and heads would nod over thick bitter ale, and all would agree that the only good gypsy was a gypsy that was swinging on the end of a rope, and that this one had better not come back if he knew what was good for him. His kind, they'd say, was the worst of what was wrong with the country; some even spoke of the return of gypsy-hunting as the best way of ridding the country of such vermin.

For Jem these words just spurred him on. 'Every evening and every night,' he said, 'I fought as if I were fighting not just for money but for my life and for the lives of all those who had gone before me.'

His was a fighting spirit he knew had been handed down through a hundred generations – a spirit tempered by a thousand years of neglect and abuse.

Go home dirty gypsis

Bastard gypsis

The words were scrawled on the wall of the Duxford Dog, scratched into the stone with sharp angular strokes. Jem paused in the alley. They'd not been there that afternoon when he'd made his way out to the Fair. He turned at a sound behind him.

The two men were red-faced with anger and drink. One was carrying a heavy stick, attached to the end of which was a curved metal blade; the other held a knife by his side. The man with the knife was swaying; the man with the stick stepped forward.

'Well now,' he said.

Jem said nothing.

The man with the stick took another step. 'I said. "Well now."'

'So?' said Jem.

The man smiled. His teeth were rotten. 'So get out of my way,' he said.

Jem turned away. Ruthie would be waiting and she didn't like waiting.

'Where are *you* going?'

He started walking. There were footsteps behind him. A hand touched his shoulder and he turned. Up close the man's face was a pattern of broken veins. His eyes were bloodshot and, when he fell and cracked the back of his head on the hard, cold ground and he lay there as still as a corpse, they stayed open, staring up at the heavens, as if he'd found there something for which he had always been searching, but the presence of which he could scarcely believe.

Next morning, when she woke, Ruthie Balls was alone. She called out but met only silence. She rose, dressed hurriedly and started searching the Fair. When nothing came of this she walked into the town and scoured the streets without success. She asked anyone she passed if they'd seen Jem. No-one had.

She found her father sitting in the sun smoking a cigar and idly watching the activity all around him. He had just finished counting last night's takings and had found them most satisfactory. As a consequence, he listened to his daughter's tearful rantings with calm detachment (after all, he knew her to be a girl given to much exaggeration) and was roused not one whit by her story. Jem, she said, was gone and was not coming back.

'Gone?' he said. 'Oh come now.'

And, she said, she was sick.

'Sick?'

It was worse, she said, when she woke. Then she touched her belly and her eyes filled with tears. In the early morning she felt a terrible sickness, adding then with a sly-looking glance at her father, that it was death late at night for which she now longed.

No-one knows for sure if the child that was born nine months later was Jem's. If he ever knew of the child's existence, Jem never spoke of it, and nor did he say why he left Mr Edward J. Balls and Sons Gentlemen's Boxing Booth. As for the man found dead in the alley outside the Duxford Dog, no-one ever came forward to claim him as their own and no-one was ever charged with his murder.

By this time, Mr Edward J. Balls appears to have developed a real affection for Jem. He tried for quite some time to find him, even employing the services of a gentleman from Norwich, whose speciality was delivering the lost into the arms of those who seek them.

'I have seen him,' the man reported, after nearly four months of silence, 'in the company of the proprietress of a certain coastal boarding-house, wherein he appears to be residing.' Which boarding-house he neglected to mention (no doubt as an aid to negotiation) and whether Jem's former employer pursued the matter is unknown. All that is clear is that the trail went cold and, in time, the Edward J. Balls and Sons Gentlemen's Boxing Booth moved on with a new Champion and then again and again, until Ruthie fell in love with a draper from Newcastle and, with her child, took his name for her own, left the Fair, becoming in time a grandmother, then a great-grandmother, finally dying at the unexpectedly advanced age of eighty-seven.

It's time to go and I'm closing the *Notes* when a slip of paper flutters out and down. I pick it up. The handwriting is old and sloping and difficult to decipher in parts.

...and sometimes months, taking rest when I can and earning food with my fiddle at the doors of distant cottages. I'd lie all day on my back in the woods or out on the open Fen, gazing up at the sky and marvelling at its blueness and the whiteness of the clouds and how some were made in the shape of faces stern or smiling and some were like islands cast adrift on the bluest of seas. Sometimes, with the warmth of the earth beneath me and the fingers of a breeze on my face I'd close my eyes and listen to the intricate workings of God's world – to the buzzing of bees and the burrowing of earthworms and the calling of songbirds in the trees, and so strongly would I feel myself a part of it that I'd begin to think that all that had happened and all that would happen signified nothing and was all just a dream. But then suddenly I'd wake and hunger and the cold and cruel world would return and so would the need for a man to find work and companions lest he disappear forever within nature's rich embrace.

Who wrote the words down for him, no-one knows. I replace the sheet and close the *Notes*. My father stirs, as if aware of my questions. But they can wait. I stand and stretch, ease back my chair. I cross the ward, and stand in silence in the lift, buttoning up my coat against the season's bitter rain.

8

HUNGER AND THE cold and cruel world forced Jem into all kinds of work, the solitude of which threatened to unsettle the very balance of his mind. He found employment as a labourer and a drayman, and as a 'snuffer' – the man who lights and extinguishes the candles in a theatre either side of an evening performance.

It was while working as a snuffer at Lincoln's Gaiety Theatre – an establishment that boasted entertainment 'of the most thrilling and melodious kind' – that his life settled into a regular and not unpleasant rhythm for a while. It was in such a place as this, one dependant on the power of fakery and the need for make-believe, that Ruthie and the face of a dead man on the cobbles lost a little sharpness and withdrew for a while – at least from the centre of his thoughts.

Indeed some nights he hardly considered the recent past at all; instead he'd sit with the stage hands in the cobbled alley that ran behind the theatre, listening to their stories of the world of the stage. He'd laugh with the working girls and drink beer, and sometimes gin, from the bottle – the latter of which he developed a taste for that would never leave him.

Then, the candles lit, he'd watch the girls in their rouge and their stained and gaudy dresses, checking their faces in the window as they waited to go on; when the show was over, he'd observe how they waited by the side door for the audience to emerge, and for a gentleman to catch their eye. It was a world of acquaintances, of temporary friends brought together by loneliness and need. It was a world in which you shared of yourself what you wanted to share and no-one asked questions, and who you were and where you'd been was no-one's business but your own.

Some nights Jem would work late, moving the wood and painted cloth backdrops in or out of the theatre, or to or from a waiting horse-drawn van. They were heavy – it could take three men to shift them. Sometimes, when the work was done, there'd be something to eat – bread, perhaps a little cold meat, a jug of beer – laid out on a table at the end of the corridor that ran between the dressing rooms, off which the theatre's manager, Mr Robinson, had his office.

Unusually for a man in his position, Mr Robinson had had no experience of the theatre as a child or even well into adulthood. The son and grandson of a doctor, he'd considered his future to be fixed: he too would become a doctor, so leaving the noble line unbroken. This, however, had been to reckon without the professionally seductive shape of Miss Janette LaSalle, a lady whose juggling abilities with a half-dozen African clubs was said, at the time, to be nothing short of legendary.

Once under her spell, a nineteen-year-old Herbert Robinson thought nothing of abandoning his studies and embarking on a life in the musical theatre. At first this took the form of following Miss LaSalle to where she might have an engagement and seeking from her an audience. This he finally achieved and, much to his surprise, what followed was a mutual declaration of love. The happy couple were married in a small Cambridge church in a ceremony attended mostly by the new Mrs Robinson's theatrical colleagues. No word of congratulation was received from either Doctor or Mrs Robinson, nor would it be until it fell to the latter to inform her son of his father's death.

Under the unaltered terms of his will, Doctor Robinson left his son the very considerable sum of seven thousand pounds. After a considerable period of genuine mourning, Henry Robinson purchased and almost completely rebuilt the Gaiety Theatre, installing, as its permanent number one attraction, Miss Janette LaSalle and her half-dozen African clubs.

Exactly what it was about Jem that so struck Mrs Robinson, one can only guess at. Undeniably he was a striking-looking young man with his dark looks and brooding manner, but he had no fortune and the rumour was that the sum of seven thousand pounds had, for Janette, been the real bridegroom at her wedding service, her husband a mere bearable necessity. Anyway, whatever it was, she was smitten.

She'd make excuses to stay at the theatre whenever Jem was working late, and she'd stand at the balcony, watching the activity below, her eyes fixed on Jem.

Jem never made it clear whether or not his attraction to Mrs Robinson was anything more than purely physical. It is also not clear if he knew anything of the child that resulted, or the children that one day would come from that child. Children like my father's grandfather.

'There's someone to see you.'

Jem lifted his head from his cot.

The tiny room was stuffy, one whole wall covered with rails of thick musty costumes.

He pushed himself up. 'Who is it?' he said.

'It's me,' said a familiar voice.

He got up, crossed to the door, turned the handle and opened it.

'Pooley stood there,' he said many years later, 'as bold as you like, his cap in his hand and the smile on his face I'd not seen for some years. Seeing him then was as strange as seeing a ghost, but as welcome as the sunshine on a cold winter's day.'

'So am I coming in?'

Without a word Jem stepped forward and the two men embraced like a pair of long lost brothers.

With his cousin's unexpected arrival Jem was thrown back into the past, the contemplation of which he'd come to consider a weakening thing – something that will sap a man's strength and stop him from moving on.

But now here was Pooley with all the news from home – how his mother missed him and still spoke of him as if he were there, all the details of who had married whom, and of the flames that had burnt down the old Cutter barn.

'It's *gone*?'

Pooley nodded.

'I can't believe it.'

The two men sat in silence as if mourning the passing of an old and dear friend.

At first Pooley was reluctant to explain just why he had arrived when he had. It was only after a visit to the ale houses of Yard Street that what he'd locked up inside him broke out and he told his cousin the truth.

'You did what?'

'I just told you.'

Jem could scarcely believe it. 'Are you telling me that it was you that burned the barn? Is that really what you're saying?'

Pooley nodded. He'd been living with the fact for so long now that hearing it put back to him it seemed quite unremarkable.

'And do they *know* it was you?'

He grinned.

'You think it's *funny?*'

'I think they got what they were owed.'

'Who did?'

'They got what they had coming. Putting up fences. Taking away the land. *Our* land.'

'You could have killed someone.'

'But I didn't.'

'That's just lucky.'

'So?'

'So what now?'

'I'm coming with you.'

'Did I say you could?'

'You're still angry.'

Jem shrugged. Anger had bled away so long ago now that it was hard to even remember it. 'I'm going back to the theatre. You can come if you want.'

Pooley smiled and slapped Jem on the shoulder, unaware that he was being watched from afar, and not kindly. 'It'll be just like the old days,' he said.

But every day is a new day and every morning a new morning and when Pooley woke to find himself snug in Jem's cot there was no sign of Jem. He sat up. His cousin's things were folded neatly on the floor.

The theatre was deserted, the auditorium dark. Pooley poked around backstage, but found nothing and no-one. He went out to the foyer. He tried the gilt-handled doors but they were locked.

Though the memory of the Cutter barn fire was distant now, the consequences of the blaze were not. So certain of the arsonist's identity had the land's new owners been that they'd sent out several men to find him. Once he'd been located, Pooley was to be returned unharmed and sent to the local assizes to have justice dispensed upon him. At the conclusion of this process, he was to be killed and his body buried where not a soul would ever find it. All this was to be done – and would be, now that the guilty man been found.

Pooley walked back through the auditorium and made his way backstage. Perhaps Jem had left a note that he had somehow over-looked. He went to Jem's room. He let himself in and began his search.

'Did you find what you were looking for?'

Pooley turned. He'd been concentrating so hard that he'd heard neither the footsteps in the hall nor the creak of the door. 'So where have you been?' he asked.

'Can't you guess?'

'Guess what?'

'How it was I got these.' Jem pulled up his shirt. There were slash-marks on his chest, red with blood. 'I can't believe you've been so stupid,' he said, wincing sharply at other unspecified wounds. 'For God's sake, why did you bring them here?'

Pooley looked down. 'I'm sorry,' he said. 'I didn't know where to go.'

'And so you came here. Brought *them* here.'

Pooley said nothing. Jem turned and walked away. He followed a few steps behind.

Of course the two men in the front stalls that night probably were just ordinary punters out for an evening of booze and girls. And when they rose at the end amid the raucous whistling and cheers, and the tall one whispered something in the shorter one's ear, it probably had nothing at all to do with Pooley and the old Cutter barn. And when an hour had passed and the theatre was quiet, and Jem was lying back in his cot, listening to Pooley's snoring and the night-sounds of the street outside, he told himself that the punches he'd thrown that afternoon in the street really had been enough to set his cousin free and clear. Here was where they'd stay. Things could go on and there'd be no more need to pick up and leave like he'd already done so many times.

But when he woke he knew differently. When he woke he knew that the men who had come for Pooley would not give up until Pooley was dead, and if someone else got in the way, well, so be it. So it was stand and fight or leave. He looked at Pooley. Pooley was a child still and knew nothing of one man's capacity to inflict pain on another. He lay back down. He listened to the distant sound of seabirds.

They walked in silence until the city was behind them and the dusk was coming on. It seemed to Jem there wasn't a place on earth he wouldn't have to leave, that there wasn't a soul whose company could really make him happy.

After days of walking they reached the coast at King's Lynn, where the Great Ouse river meets the Wash. Here they found work on one of the old coal barges that made their lumbering way along the coast as far as Ipswich in the south and Skegness in the north. It was dirty work and harder than anything either of them had ever done. But it was out on the water, where not a soul could ever find them.

9

BEING TOLD THAT your mother is alive (and, indeed, that by taking so long to find a parking space you've only just missed her), when you know for a fact that she died nearly six years ago, is something for which one is never prepared.

'*Who?*' you say and 'No, you must be mistaken.' Neither response seems to work, however. And if you happen to mention the fact of her actual *death*, then those who thought you merely unlucky now think you mad or callous, and wish at once to protect from you the information's source.

In this case my father – a man married happily to, it seems, a ghost.

Of course he's gone when I get there, and there's no-one around to tell me to where. Sunday, and the place is deserted more than ever. I sit down. I stand up. I feel so terribly agitated. I want to say, *What the hell are you saying to these people about my mother?* But then, in a quite unexpected moment of clearsightedness, it comes to me.

It's her.

She's here. That woman.

'Hello?'

The nurse is smiling; her hand finds my shoulder.

'Where is he?' I say.

The smile fades. She clearly dislikes my tone. 'If you mean your father, he's down in the dining-room.'

'The dining-room? I thought he couldn't walk to the toilet.'

'Not without assistance, no.'

'So he has *assistance* now?'

'Clearly.' The nurse lifts a page on her clipboard. She makes a brutal mark with her pen then turns and is gone.

Assistance.

I wait half an hour. Three quarters. I stand in the corridor and drop a coin in the phone box.

'Hello?' My wife's voice seems distant.

'Look,' I say, 'you'll never guess what he's done...' But something makes me stop. 'What is it?' I say. 'What's happened?'

I listen, but her words seem to come out all jumbled. I set down the phone. *Oh God oh God.*

———————

Captain Henry Harriott of the sailing barge *Endeavour* knew better than most why a man would seek a life on the water. Whilst a man could simply love the smell of it or be fit for nothing else, it was in his experience most likely that such a man was running from something and needed a place to hide. It was why he as a young man had sought the emptiness of the sea and why for nearly thirty years now the *Endeavour* had been his home.

———————

'Well?'

My wife sits beside me, exhausted. Silence, and then, 'How can you read at a time like this?'

I shrug. Glance at the page.

A sailing barge of the time.

'It takes my mind off things,' I say. I feel her turn to me, await her anger.

'Your son,' she says, 'is lying ten feet away and you're trying to take your mind off things? He could die and you're reading?'

'He won't die,' I say. 'It's a broken wrist.'

'Are you a doctor?' she says.

I say *No, of course not.* I put my hand on her leg. She pulls away, stands up.

'I'm going for some air,' she says.

I watch her go, hear the swoosh of the automatic door. I look around. I expect accusing looks but find none. I look down at the page.

A sailing barge of the time.

I feel like crying.

A sailing barge of the time had, besides the captain, a crew of four. Its work was simple and monotonous, consisting of the picking up, transporting and delivering of coal from King's Lynn to Skegness and back. This routine involved negotiating the contradictory currents of the Wash, which, while never dramatic in appearance, had enough about them to surprise even the most experienced sailor.

Why Captain Harriott took the two cousins on no-one knows. They had no experience of the sea (Pooley had never even *seen* it) and there was no shortage of labour. Enclosure of the land and the slow creep of mechanization meant that each day more and more young men found themselves without work, and so in search of something that would keep them alive. Some headed for the cities, others for the coast. And while, to Captain Harriott, Jem and Pooley must have seemed like all the others, for some reason he chose them.

Setting out from King's Lynn on a cold and squally day they could still make out the Stump far away across the water. The Stump was the spire of Boston Parish Church, the point by which so much navigation on the Wash is achieved. The barge heavy with coal, they moved slowly through the water, all the time hugging the coast while the fishing boats headed further out in search of shrimp and cockles and muscles. Overhead against the flat grey sky, oystercatchers and dunlin and common terns arched and wheeled, while the gulls screeched and dove upon the small boats, scavenging for scraps.

It was just another early morning for the sailors on the Wash – and another day of sickness for Pooley.

'Lay down and it'll kill you, boy.'

But this time he couldn't get up. It was worse even than yesterday. Everyone had kept telling him he'd get used to it and that the sickness and the pressure in his head would cease. But he hadn't got used to it and he knew he never would. He howled as the *Endeavour* rose and fell again, and hung his head over the side of the bunk. The sick spewed from him until there was no more.

Henry Harriott shook his head. He'd seen novices go green and all kinds of sickness but he'd never seen such a strong man so unable to shake it. 'It's no use,' he said. Pooley tried to look up. 'Some people just aren't fit for it.'

When Pooley woke he felt like he'd sicked up his entire insides. He looked over to Jem's bunk.

Jem turned. 'Well, at least you're alive,' he said.

'I don't feel like it,' said Pooley.

'What will you do?'

'I don't know.' He turned onto his back and sighed. After a while he said, 'Did you ever hear of a man called Nat Langham?'

'I did,' said Jem. 'Why?'

'Did you know he's staying in Yarmouth?'

'So?'

'So, you're a fighter.'

'*Was.*'

'So maybe you should fight.'

'I *was* a fighter.'

'And maybe you should see this Nat Langham.'

'Why would he see me?'

'Because it's his business. To find the next Champion of the World.'

Jem turned his head. 'You're worse than I thought,' he said. 'They should throw you overboard.'

'And you should use what God gave you,' said Pooley, as another wave of nausea rolled up and over him like the tide.

It was dusk when Jem woke. Whether a minute or an hour had passed he couldn't say. Pooley's bunk was empty. Still half in the fog of sleep, Jem tried to think what this meant. Perhaps he'd gone into Skegness, or maybe he was just up on deck taking the air.

Jem climbed the steps to find that the wind had dropped and the water was flat and still, as the night settled in. He walked from stern to bow and back. There was no sign of Pooley. He looked to the quayside. Everything was quiet.

'Hey Jem...' Pooley's voice was distant and it took Jem a while to find where it was coming from. At last he did – a small figure at the end of the cobbled lane that led up from the quayside and into the town. The figure raised his arm in a wave; before turning away, walking up the cobbles. And then he was gone.

Jem thought about going after him but knew it would make no difference – leaving was what Pooley did, and nothing could change that. Instead he went back down below and lay on his rough bunk.

He thought of Pooley and Beeston and the old Cutter barn and he thought of his sick and dying father and everything he'd left so far behind. And he thought of Nat Langham and the old hope rose once again inside him. He tried to sleep but couldn't. In his mind, once again, he was Champion of the World.

'I'll have to let you go.'

'*Go?*' said Jem.

'I can't pay you any more. If you've any sense you'll take work on the railway. Boats are dying.'

Captain Harriott raised an arm as the *Endeavour* pulled away. He called out but his words were whipped away by the wind, and soon he and his boat were gone for good.

Jem sat on the quayside and took out his fiddle. Soon a small group had gathered to listen – fishermen and coalmen and women on their way to buy and sell at the market. They stood and listened to the young man's mournful tunes and were taken back to an earlier time for a while. But then a steam horn rent the air and the spell was broken. The crowd dispersed, returning to the stunted, brutal business of their lives.

For Jem there was nothing to do now but return to the road. This time, though, it was different. This time, for the first time in years, he knew where he was going. This time there was a man he had to meet, the glimmer of a future to seize.

'Shouldn't you tell him?'

'Tell him what?'

'That we're here. That his grandson's here.'

'Why?'

She shrugs.

'Precisely.'

In a while she looks down at the *Notes*. 'What are you going to do with those?'

'I don't know. Nothing probably.'

'Did you ask him why he gave them to you?'

'Nope.'

'Don't you think you should?'

Just then a different nurse appears. She is smiling, which we take to mean good news.

'Is my boy alright?' I say.

'See for yourself.'

He's sitting up, his tiny wrist in a soft caste. His face is pale. He has dark circles under his eyes.

'He was very brave,' says the nurse, ruffling his hair.

In the car going home he's very quiet, like there's something on his mind. I try to lighten things up but nothing works. I turn on the radio.

'Do we have to?' says his mother.

I turn it off.

It's not for another week or so that he tells me what's been bothering him.

'You know Grandad,' he says.

Yes, I say, I know Grandad.

'Well,' he says, 'when he dies will he see Grannie again?'

'You mean in Heaven?' I say.

He nods.

Of course I tell him *Yes*. Of course I don't say that if Heaven does exist then there's no chance they'll let *him* in.

'I'm glad,' he says, as he snuggles down for sleep.

'I love you,' I say and I kiss the top of his beautiful head. I cross the room and close the door quietly.

Tonight there's a moon. It spills its silver light across the lawn, illuminating for a moment the high-stepping trot of a fox.

On the morning of 2nd May 1845, a crowd of young children was gathered by their teachers in the middle of Great Yarmouth's suspension bridge to help celebrate its completion: as part of the festivities a clown was to be pulled down the River Yare in a barrel by a flock of tethered geese. As the barrel passed beneath the new bridge the children moved from one side to the other in order to watch its progress, so fatally shifting the distribution of weight, and causing the chains on the south side of the bridge to give way. As a consequence, the whole thing collapsed, sending seventy-seven children and two teachers to their deaths in the river below. It was the greatest tragedy ever to visit the town and is still remembered today. Every year on its anniversary, a prayer is said at St Nicholas' Church and candles lit – seventy-nine of them – in memory of those lost.

Also noteworthy is the fact that the town's monument to Nelson, built to celebrate his victory at the Battle of the Nile, faces not outward towards the sea as you might expect, but inland. It is said to have been a mistake by the builders, chief amongst whom was a Frenchman. Whatever the truth, it was here, beneath this monument that Jem took his rest when at last he arrived in the half-slum, half-genteel town of Great Yarmouth. And it was here, in this small seaside town, that his life would take the turn that would change the rest of his life.

But *then*, as he passed through a gate in the old Roman wall, he knew none of this. *Then*, as he headed for the market-place, he neither knew where he was going nor what he would do when he got there.

The town behind South Quay was and is still a maze of alleys. Called the Rows, today they are gentrified; in the 1850s they were the haunt of the town's underclass – the whores and pickpockets, the thugs and wasters, the sick, the poor and the downright mad. It was to this place that, soon after his arrival, Jem found his way.

———

'What were you doing?'

'What do you think?'

'I thought I heard someone outside.'

'There's a moon,' I say.

'So?'

'So nothing.'

I slip into bed, pick up the *Notes*. She turns over, away. Such disengagement is my father's doing.

I turn the page. *He lived in those first few days,* I read. I try not to think. Night is no time for thinking.

He lived in those first few days by means of his fiddle, playing shanties and laments on street-corners and outside the town's many raucous pubs.

All thoughts at night are dark, black.

I sit up, clean the smudges from my glasses. I settle them again, read on.

———•—•———

Located in the Marine Parade, the Growler public house had long been the favoured location in the town for cockfighting and, consequently (the presence of one brutal and illegal pastime inviting another), the bloody art of bare-knuckle boxing. All of which excited the shallow bravado of the pampered sons of merchants and those of more aristocratic birth, for whom the slim risk of arrest had its own delicious allure.

The three men were drunk. They stumbled from the Snug Bar, foul-mouthed and wreaking of beer. The largest of them – seeing the fiddle-player with his dark eyes and olive skin – chose in his drunkenness to call the man's mother *Gypsy whore*, and to raise his fist and smash the man's fiddle and stamp it into a hundred pieces. They didn't know that they'd found a man so weary and so longing for something he'd not yet found that he had nothing left to lose.

Never in my life did I fight so gladly or with feelings of more bitter animosity. They had smashed my fiddle and I meant to smash them.

And he did – and when it was over and the small crowd that had gathered on the sea-front had drifted away and the cheering was gone, Jem stooped to pick up what was left of his fiddle. He didn't know that his life would never be the same again – that the tall disfigured man in the London dandy's suit who was smoking a cigar and leaning most casually against the wall of the pub was the man who would change everything.

Smiling, the man raised his cigar.

'Who are you?' said Jem.

The gentleman in the fine suit half-frowned. 'You don't know me?' he said. There was a distant kind of mockery in his voice.

'Should I?'

The man shrugged. 'Because everyone knows me. And anyone who doesn't doesn't matter.'

'Well I don't.'

'Well that's a shame. But that can change.'

'Look,' said Jem. 'I don't know you and I don't *want* to know you.'

The tall man smiled. 'You will,' he said. 'You will.' Then, his cigar gripped tight between his teeth, he turned and walked away, his leather boots clipping sharp on the cobbles.

With the man gone Jem retrieved what remained of his fiddle. He carried the shards of broken wood and what was left of the strings to the quayside and tossed them into the water. They floated away on the outgoing tide. He stood and watched them until they were gone.

10

THE SCARRING WAS terrible, the boy's mouth red and raw for months, his left cheek twisted and disfigured. Women looked away when they saw him and men just stared as if at some strange creature in a zoo. The effect diminished as he grew, but it was always there, always a reminder of the poverty of his youth and the desperate unending search for food.

By the age of seven, Nat Langham was an accomplished survivor. He knew every twist and turn of the slum streets of Leicester's Hinkley district and the best ways to avoid a pursuer. If cornered he knew how to fight and he knew that if you fight then you don't stop fighting until the other man is begging for mercy and will never raise a challenge again. He learned on those dark, stinking streets that eating is not a right, and that a simple potato could mean the difference between another day's scavenging or another cold corpse bought for a shilling and laid out for dissection before an audience of doctors at the Leicester Infirmary.

A potato.

Life and death.

So that day he'd reached up and wrapped his gloved hand around the hot prize and run as fast as he could, but then he stumbled and he fell to the ground, and Mr Sawyer the Potato Man was over him, his face red with anger.

He reached down and forced the boy's mouth open, then jammed in the boiling hot potato. The boy screamed and screamed but then he was silent. Then the night was coming on and when the boy opened his eyes he thought he must have died and gone to Heaven as the pain was gone and everything was numb and it was like he was floating and no longer in agony.

But then the pain returned and nothing would stop it. People looked at him and laughed, and when he looked at himself in a mirror he cried. He was seven years old but might as well have been dead.

The man's body was found on a patch of waste ground on the edge of Cross Keys. Although badly burned, it was soon identified as the body of Frederic Sawyer, a street vendor. Although in those days death in the streets was quite unremarkable, there was one feature of the murder that aroused great local interest. It appeared that the victim's mouth had been wedged open by a large potato, which thanks to the cause of death had been cooked inside and out to perfection.

They say any gentleman who found himself alone in the Rows was either a fool or belonged there. Which description best fitted Nat Langham was difficult to say. He spoke with an accent that was far from local and had a way about him that told you he was different. In no time word went around that he was looking for someone and would be willing to pay handsomely for any information. In the end all it cost him was four shillings – a sum he was happy to pay. It was a bargain when set against the fortune he was certain could be made.

'Do you know me now?' he said.

'Only from yesterday.'

They were standing in Killywitches Row, the object of much curiosity.

'My name is Nat Langham.'

'I know.'

'Two pounds a week all told. What do you say?'

'What?'

'That's my offer.'

'What for?'

'You. So get your things and come with me.'

'Where?'

'You'll see.'

'No.'

'One minute.'

'What?'

'And then I go and I don't come back.'

'You're mad.'

'Half a minute.'

'What?'

'Twenty seconds.'

'All right, all right,' said Jem. 'I'm coming.'

The Royal Hotel was the very last building on the Great Yarmouth sea-front heading south. By far the grandest of the town's many hotels, it was the favourite of the wealthy and had on three separate occasions played host to Her Majesty the Queen. To Jem it was somewhere from another world – a world where the food on your plate was too plentiful to eat, one where comfort and warmth were simple fact and not fantasy.

'Yes, sir. Of course, sir.' The desk clerk spun the book on the high-polished counter. 'If the *gentleman* would care to sign the register...'

Jem looked at the pen held towards him. He stared at the book, at the jumble of neatly sloping marks.

'Allow me,' said Nat Langham.

'Of course,' said the desk clerk, with what Jem was certain was a sneer.

'You see my friend here,' said Nat Langham, 'is the next Champion of the World and needs to take care of his hands.' He glanced at Jem. 'Isn't that right?'

Jem watched his name – *James Mace Esq* – added to the list in the book. He knew the shapes, of course, but not the way they could be turned into sounds.

Nat Langham spun the book back. 'One day,' he said smiling at the desk clerk, 'you'll be telling your children of this day. If, that is, you find a whore drunk enough to receive your attentions.'

'I beg your—'

Directed by a strong hand, Jem turned away from the desk and was guided to the stairs, aware as he went of the desk clerk's outraged eyes upon him.

The room was vast – it was two rooms, in fact – a bedroom and a sitting room, either one of which was bigger than the whole cottage in Beeston. There were upholstered chairs and polished tables and a bed so large and deep that it seemed a man could quite easily get lost in it. There were flowers in huge vases before each window. Beyond the glass, down below, lay a terrace set with two dozen chairs and tables, then a neat grass verge and a cleanly-swept promenade, along which gentlemen and their ladies strolled in the hour before noon. And beyond all this, beyond the evidence of wealth and repose, lay the primitive sea, restless and ever-moving, stretching further away than the eye could ever see or the mind imagine.

Jem sat in every chair and looked in every cupboard, all of which were empty save a single copy of the Bible. He lay back on the bed and opened it at random, but, of course, could make no sense of it. He laid it down and closed his eyes. He listened to the sound of distant voices and the calling of the gulls as they swooped and scavenged.

The next Champion of the World.

He tried to picture the future but could not. Instead he took refuge in the past.

Once, as a boy, he'd sneaked into Mr Stephenson's back yard, to get a close look at his famous fighting dogs. At first, thanks to the bright June sun, he'd not seen them lying quiet in the shadows. But then he'd heard their breathing. There'd been four of them curled up together in a great mass of matted fur and jutting limbs. He'd stood for a while just watching them – the rise and gentle fall of their breathing, the way they twitched and muttered as they dreamed – unable to see in them the viciousness and bloodlust with which they'd been bred to perform.

11

HE COUGHS AT night like a colic child but it seems that no-one hears him but me. Only I am woken by the sound and only I am driven to push myself out of bed and into my slippers and dressing-gown, making my way down the stairs by the nightlight's blue glow and across the hall to the kitchen. I don't turn on the light for fear it will scare him away. Instead, like an old man who's losing his sight, I shuffle about in the darkness, chopping up scraps retrieved from the bin and scraping them into a bowl.

I understand from my on-line enquiries that a fox will only eat the food you give him if he is forced to dig for it. To this end I have dug a small hole in the centre of the lawn into which every night I place the metal bowl. This then I cover with dirt. I then return to the house and my place here by the kitchen window. Sometimes I have to wait for hours for Mr Fox to arrive and sometimes he doesn't come at all. Whichever it is, it gives me time to go on with the *Notes*. Why this has become so important to me I have no idea, although I cannot escape the feeling that there is something in them for me – that some-thing will be made clear if I only read on. So I do.

'Aren't you going to work?' she says.

As I did last night.

'I called in.'

'Again?'

'I've things to do.'

'Well *I* have to go in. *Someone* has to.'

'And someone has to be here. *With our son.*'

'Well then that would be *you* obviously.'

In a while I hear the front door close and go to check on our son. He is sleeping, his poorly arm resting on the bedclothes. His breath is shallow but even. I close the door quietly and return to the kitchen. I make some coffee and sit at the table, as has become my routine. Before me are the *Notes*. I turn the pages, begin again the search for what they may or may not be trying to tell me.

———•———

For one thing, Nat Langham was the only man ever to beat Tom Sayers. He won the contest in sixty rounds – nearly blinding the man in the process with the savagery of his punches. Soon after, he retired in order to concentrate on where the real money lay. The real money wasn't in boxing but in *boxers*. The real money was sitting idle in the pockets of gentlemen with far too much of it; to have them give it up would be about as simple as picking their pockets.

When he bought it, The Cambrian Stores was a down-at-heel sporting pub on London's St Martin's Lane. When he'd finished with it, when the walls had been painted, the floors laid with carpet and intricate glasswork installed to give the place class – it looked so grand that he had to buy a whole new set of clothes to match it. He would stand by the oak bar and smell the new paint. Not bad for a boy from the slums of Cross Keys.

The Rum-Pum-Pas Club it was called, the name derived from the sound of a fist striking flesh. Beneath the gilded ceiling, he'd built a canvas-floored, roped-off ring. Forty-five linen-dressed tables were set around the ring; in the centre of each sat a candle in a wrought-iron holder. The food and drink available were equally fine.

Within a month the club was full every night, the air thick with cigars and the laughter of young, moneyed gentlemen. At ten o'clock every night, dressed for the occasion in a gleaming tuxedo, Nat would announce the evening's entertainment for the pleasure of those in attendance.

The fighters came from all over the country – the result of Nat's roaming – the slums of any town the places to find them. He knew that a certain sum of money lay in each protégé. Some would last a single fight, others long enough to become Champion themselves. First, though, for all was the apprenticeship.

The Langham Booth was a feeder for the Rum-Pum-Pas. It toured the country giving exhibitions in the art of fistiana, its arrival announced by the appearance of posters attached to trees and the walls of public buildings the night before. This job had been Jem's – as it had been each of the apprentices' – first task. He'd carry his bundle of posters and a hammer and nails, and slip through the shadows, pausing here and there to perform his sneaky task. To be caught meant an appearance before the magistrate, which could be followed by a term of imprisonment. You had to be fast and you had to be fearless, for those who *did* fail were abandoned to their fate. It was brutal, but so was life.

Some like Jem were special. Some rose through the ranks at what seemed to others a quite indecent rate.

'So do you care the others dislike you?'

Jem said that no, he didn't care.

It was early morning on the outskirts of Bristol. Jem had been Champion for a month.

Nat knew it was a lie. No man, he knew, can stand silence from his peers for too long. 'Good,' he said. 'I'm glad to hear it. Because you're coming with me.'

'Where?' said Jem as if he didn't know.

Arriving in London at Christmas was like arriving at the centre of the world – which, in those days, it was. With Victoria already twenty years on the throne, the city was the centre of the largest empire the world had ever known – a bustling, self-important, genteel slum of a city. There were trains that ran in tunnels underground and buildings so tall that they seemed to touch the sky. It was dirty and foul-smelling, a place where a man must keep his money close and his eyes wide open. For Jem it was the scariest thing he'd ever seen.

It was dark when the horse-drawn cab pulled up in St Martin's Lane. They seemed to have driven for hours, crossing bridges and passing along streets, each dressed in the thickest of snow, as if for his arrival. The snow was falling still when they crossed the bustling road and slipped unnoticed into the club.

Nat leaned over and said something that Jem couldn't hear above the noise.

'I said, "What do you think?"'

Jem shook his head. Nat nodded towards the far corner of the room. Jem followed him through the smoke and the crowd, aware only, as he drew close to it, of the presence of the boxing ring and the fighters above him, and the sweat and the blood and the champagne and the fine suits, and all he so longed for.

Nat's office was dark oak and leather. A fire was raging in the grate. Above the mantle was a crude portrait of a pale, muscled man. The man was stripped to the waist, his fists held out before him in the classic fighter's pose.

'Do you know who that is?' Nat was easing back in his chair, a cigar in his mouth, his feet on the desk, the polish of his boots catching the flickering of the fire.

'No,' said Jem. 'Should I?'

'You don't know much do you?'

'Enough.'

'Is enough enough?'

Jem shrugged.

Nat swung in his chair, dropped his feet and sat forward. 'How's tomorrow night sound?' he said.

'It sounds good,' said Jem. He was suddenly so tired that all he wanted to do was sleep.

'Well do you?'

He looked up. 'What?'

'Aren't you listening to me?'

'Yes.'

'Then you'd have heard me asking if you understood.'

'Understood.'

'The rules. The rule.'

Jem said yes, he understood. You fight. You win.

Nat Langham replaced his cigar and sat back in his chair. 'Tomorrow night then,' he said. 'And remember. I only look after winners. Lose and you'll be back where I found you. Do you understand *now*?'

'And when I win,' said Jem. 'What then?'

'Then you do it again.'

'Then what?'

'Again.'

'And then?'

'And then we get you a chair and a nice big cigar and you say, "Thanks Mr Langham." And when I'm old and the thing that's going to get me finally gets me and I can see the way home, I'll say, "That boy was a Champion and it's all because of me." Now, was there anything else?'

'I need somewhere to stay.'

'Speak to Lewis. Tell him to give you the key to the Champion's suite.'

'What?'

'And when you've done that will you leave me alone? I have money to count and places I have to go to spend it.'

⎯⎯•⎯⎯

The thing that's going to get me.

It's always a bus – always the same bus.

For my father this was always what would get him. 'I can picture it now', he would say, 'turning out of the Kingston bus depot', and he'd describe to a small boy how that bus had his name on the front and no matter what you do if its got your name on it then you've had it. 'Sooner or later,' he'd say, 'you won't see it coming and it'll run you right over.'

Which, of course, didn't happen. There was no bus and no accident. Just an old heart running down to the point at which it could stop at any minute.

I turn the page. The doorbell rings. An Eastern European man selling cleaning products. I buy two dusters and a tin of polish. Is it, I want to ask, *Polish* polish? but I decide against it. It might make me seem unbalanced. Besides he probably gets it all the time. I close the door and look at the clock. An hour to go till the boy's medicine.

⎯⎯•⎯⎯

Freezing in winter and boiling in summer, the Champion's suite was an attic room with one small window that looked out west across the city. It was tiny, the sloping ceiling making it awkward to stand up. There was a bed and a table upon which stood a jug and a washing bowl. The jug was chipped, the curtains frayed and faded. There was a single hook on the back of the door. The floor was bare boards.

Jem opened the window and leaned out. The air was cold and

sharp, the sky clear. The stars were less bright above the city – or perhaps just further away. The pavements were white with snow, people hurrying this way and that, each one concerned only with his own narrow world. He watched a small boy on the corner selling newspapers and thought suddenly of his parents and the summers spent with Pooley in the dusty lanes of Beeston.

Jem woke to find ice on the inside of the window and his breath coming thick as smoke in the attic's chilled air. He lay still, listening to the distant noises in the street and the occasional sound of voices on the stairs.

The Club at that hour was deserted. He was hungry so he made his way to the kitchen. He called out. Nothing. He found some bread and a long, curved knife. There was ham and a little cheese.

It was midday when he heard a key turning in a lock. He crept out of the kitchen to see. The man was locking the street-door behind him; then he turned and set down a carpet-bag. He shook off his shabby coat and folded it over the back of a chair.

'Who's there?' he called out when he heard a creak. He was pale-faced, his eyes set in deep dark hollows.

Jem stepped out and introduced himself.

The man shrugged, weary. 'I suppose he gave you the attic.'

'Yes, what of it?'

'Nothing.'

The man's name was Elke. 'Like the deer,' he said as he'd said a thousand times. He paused. 'You beat Slasher, right?'

'Yes,' said Jem.

'Did you know he killed a man? Cut him in two with a butcher's knife?'

'I heard that wasn't true.'

'It was true. I was there. Saw it with my own eyes.'

'Well I beat him anyway.'

'So you did.'

Robert Elke smiled. 'You and I will be friends,' he said.

'How do you know?'

'Trust me.'

Jem shrugged.

And so they were. From that day on Robert Elke was never far from Jem's side – he would be there, in fact, until the day he fell down drunk on a Toronto street and a horse kicked him so hard in the back that it broke his spine and killed him.

But that was all years ahead. The horse that would kill him had yet to be born and the existence of Toronto was still unknown to both men.

'So what do you use?'

'What do you mean?' said Jem.

'On your hands. What do you use? You must use something.'

Jem looked down at his hands.

Robert Elke leaned forward and took Jem's right hand in his. The knuckles were solid and swollen. 'You'll be finished in a year,' he said.

'What?'

'Unless you do as you're told. Unless you soak them. And you have to take care of them like they were precious. If you don't you'll lose them, and what else have you got?'

Jem said nothing. He was stretching and bunching his fingers.

'Come with me,' said Robert Elke. Jem followed him into the back room.

What he knew about the body Robert Elke had gained solely from observation and experience. He knew, for example, that a man wracked with back pain shouldn't just lie in his bed and wait for it to pass, but exercise to prevent a general seizing up. He knew also that to bleed a man who is already weak is to weaken him further, and that a woman in labour should, on no account, drink gin in large quantities. It was knowledge that, combined with a terrible loss in the ring, which had crippled his health forever, turned him from a fighter to the best corner man any man could desire. That it was Nat Langham who had beaten him and now employed him was, for Robert Elke, a source of neither shame nor pride; it was simply the way things were.

Jem was lying on his bed when he heard someone climbing the stairs. He sat up and swung his legs to the floor.

'Jem?'

'What is it? Is it time?'

'It's time,' said Robert Elke peering in. 'How are your hands?'

Jem looked at them, turned them over. 'Ugly,' he said.

'Match the rest of you then.'

The combination of alcohol and gunpowder had turned them a dark mulatto brown. He bunched them into fists. 'What's it like being old?' he said.

Robert Elke shrugged. 'You piss more and sleep less. Why?'

Jem shrugged.

'Look,' said Robert Elke. 'Are you coming or not?'

'Yes,' said Jem.

'Well, let's go then.'

'My heart was thumping hard,' he later dictated, 'as we drew nearer to the crowd. I stretched my fingers, then made them into fists and tried to think of Pooley and what he would have said if he'd been there to see me now. But he wasn't there, and though he wasn't there I wasn't alone.'

The fight was short and brutal, Jem's opponent, a young aristocrat by the name of Lord Drumlarig soundly beaten, his white ruffled shirt soon drenched in his own blood. He'd fought on with a smile on his pale handsome face and when forced to retire had shaken Jem by the hand and offered him two sovereigns.

'Gentlemen,' he'd said, 'this novice of Nat's is too good for me. Is there perhaps amongst you other "pros" someone who might give him more of a contest?'

And there was – but none of them lasted long. Even Johnny Walker, who, in his prime, had beaten men like Fred Mason, Sam Simmonds and Neil Adams, was forced to retire in less than nineteen minutes, his left eye cut and swollen, and his breath coming hard.

Later that night, Jem was sitting in the backroom eating roast beef and plum pudding, when Nat Langham appeared. There was, he said, someone who wished to make his acquaintance. He stepped back and opened the door and in walked a small, thin boy.

'Hello,' said Jem, rising, 'and who are you?'

The boy looked down.

'This,' said Nat Langham, 'is a friend of mine. Alfred Douglas, Lord Drumlarig's only son. Alfred, meet Jem Mace, the next Champion of the World.'

The boy reached out a pale hand and shook Jem's. He was a boy, who, in later years, Jem would come to know well, for, on the death of his father, Alfred Douglas would become both the new Lord Drumlarig and the ninth Marquess of Queensbury. He'd be a man famous not only for the rules of boxing he would one day introduce, but also for the destruction he would bring down on the brilliant, fragile life of Oscar Wilde.

12

BY THE YEAR of 1857 there were two thousand, eight hundred and twenty-five brothels recorded within the boundaries of the city of London. Of that total, eighty per cent were located in the capital's maritime areas, the remaining twenty per cent in the East and West Ends. In those days, the East End was one vast slum with open running sewers and a population of rats far outnumbering the human inhabitants, and its brothels were consequently filthy. Those located in the West End, around Leicester Square and Haymarket, were less so, their moneyed clientele demanding higher standards from their vice, both in terms of cleanliness and the decor of their surroundings. One such place was the Baker Mews Ladies' Club, the interior of which resembled a pasha's boudoir, complete with low-lying ottomans, hookahs belching forth heavy-scented smoke and a thousand yards of velvet drapery. A regular visitor (Jem would be loaned out as bodyguard to the more important clients of the Rum-Pum-Pas, many of whom had long-standing accounts at the Ladies' Club), Jem was well known not only to the club's owners but also to most of the cabbies and doormen who made their livings in this part of the city. It was through his association with the latter that, on many occasions, he was able to sneak in through a theatre's side door and take up any available unsold seat.

It was during a visit to Mr Fox Cooper's City of London Theatre at Bishopsgate, while Jem was following the progress of Oliver Twist, and Fagin, Nancy and the terrible Bill Sykes, that a hand found his shoulder and a voice in his ear suggested with some determination that he might care to step outside. This he did, all the time expecting an attempted arrest and a need to run for it, until, once out in the street, the man who'd expelled him introduced himself with a flourish. His name, he said, was Charles Dickens.

'So?'

'Have you not heard of me?'

'No.'

The short man with the wild hair seemed perplexed.

'Look…' said Jem.

'I was told you were in the house tonight. I was intrigued to meet you.'

'What do you want?'

'I don't want anything.'

Jem turned away and pushed the door.

'What is it?'

'It's closed.'

'You could try the front entrance.'

Jem hesitated. He had money in his pocket but not enough to waste getting back into somewhere he'd got in for free. 'I'm going,' he said.

'Going? Don't you want to know how it ends?'

He shrugged.

'Don't you *care*? What about Nancy?'

'What *about* her? Who are you?'

'I wrote what you have been watching.'

Jem frowned

'I created them all. They wouldn't exist but for me.'

'I see,' said Jem. 'So what are you doing here?'

'Watching over them.'

'But they're not real.'

'Then,' said the other man, 'I have failed.'

'That's a good coat.'

'What?'

'Must have cost a fortune.'

He looked down at his coat as if surprised to find it there. He pushed back the collar and slipped it off. 'It's yours,' he said.

'What?'

'Take it.'

Jem stepped back as if the man were a villain and the coat a pointed stick. 'I just meant it must be good to fail in such luxury.'

'I know what you meant.'

'I don't need your coat.'

'I know.'

'So put it back on.'

'Very well.' He did.

'I have to go,' said Jem.

'May I walk with you?'

'Why?'

'Indulge me.'

'It's a long way.'

'I'll try to keep up.'

Jem shook his head. The man was quite clearly mad. 'It's up to you,' he said, and off he went, aware of silence behind him for a second, and then the sound of following footsteps.

He'd been matched to fight the great Bill Thorpe on a piece of wasteland near the mouth of the Medway River in Kent. It was a step up from the Rum-Pum-Pas but illegal in the eyes of the law. Nat offered Jem fifty pounds in the knowledge that, should his man prevail, then *his* prize would run over time into thousands.

First, though, Jem had to be prepared. He was overweight and in need of greater stamina. Bring on the dog-cart and horse-hair towels.

The subject of this process was attached to a dog-cart and the dogs whipped so hard that they'd run like crazy, so forcing the poor soul to follow. If he stumbled and fell he'd be dragged along the street (it was always in the streets and always under cover of darkness) until something – anything – stopped him. It was brutal but it kept a man in shape. Then there was skipping and weights and a daily rubbing down with horse-hair towels that would sting like nettles and smart the muscles into life, and the copperas, whiskey, gunpowder and horseradish concoction with which his hands – but not just his hands – were prepared. His face too would be painted with a brush, so turning it in time 'quite as black as a negro's'. Only then, when all this and more had been done, was he ready.

The day of the fight was a glorious one – more May than February – allowing all those present to remove their tail-coats and their gleaming top-hats, and lounge with their champagne and hampers in the long grass at the edge of the ring. It was a guinea to get in and a further two to ensure no police interference.

On the stroke of ten o'clock the fighters were ready. Jem ducked down beneath the rope and rose; his employer held him back.

'Just remember,' Nat said, 'there's two thousand pounds riding on this, so don't you dare lose, do you hear me?'

Jem nodded. He knew it was victory or nothing – and not just victory. It had to be a victory so emphatic – a beating so complete – that no-one would ever dare stand in his way. Lose it, he knew, and everything would be over. He was fighting for his life.

It took seventeen rounds but he won and won well. He knocked Big Bill Thorpe all over the ring with a ferocity that surprised even Robert Elke and made many in the crowd let their champagne go flat. It was such a battering that some wanted it stopped before the older man was murdered, but nothing could stop it, and on and on it went until Big Bill Thorpe was a bloody, crumpled mass, who would never fight again in his lifetime. His nose was broken and his spirit too. He was taken from the ring to a chorus of boos.

'Hey Jem!'

He turned amid the jostling back-slapping crowd. It was Pooley.

'You did it, Jem.'

Jem smiled the broadest of smiles. Blood was running down his face, but in that moment he didn't care. 'What are you doing here?' he called out.

'I've met a girl, Jem.'

'What?' It was hard to hear above the noise.

'A girl. We're getting married.'

'Married?'

'I've come to get you.'

'I can't hear you.'

'I said, I've come to fetch you. You're to be my best man...'

But then arms hoisted Jem up and the flow of the crowd took him off. He turned back to find his cousin, but he was gone, lost amid the chaos and excitement of victory.

The two were to be married in the spring of that year in the bride-to-be's hometown of Leicester. According to Pooley, his fiancée was both sweet and feisty, the daughter of a wool merchant, to whom family was everything and its protection by any means necessary his sacred duty.

The last resting place of King Richard III and the home of Joseph Aloysius Hansom, inventor of the cab of that name, the city of

Leicester had become, by the time of Jem and Pooley's arrival for the wedding, not only the centre of the East Midlands knitting industry, but also the high watermark of the cholera epidemic that had been sweeping the towns and villages of that part of the country with such awful speed that scarcely a soul had remained untouched.

Number 266 London Road (now a part of DeMontfort University) was a neat, modest home in an area of town thought to be on the rise. Solidly built in the local red brick, it spoke of permanence, of inviobility: *here we are*, it seemed to say, *and here we stay.*

They arrived by train one morning in May, the two cousins having no idea of the tragedy awaiting them. As they strolled along the London Road in the sunshine, talking of weddings and romance and where they would be in a year from now, they failed to notice the sombre tone of the streets around them, or the number of curtains still drawn at eleven. Even the racecourse that day was as quiet as a tomb. It wasn't until they were walking up the path and they heard the gate close behind them with a satisfying *click* that something told them all was not as it should be. The simple black wreath attached to the door spoke of the presence of death.

'Pooley raised his hand to the door,' Jem said, many years later, 'intending with a knock to gain entry to the house of his beloved, but his fist froze in the air. He asked me what had happened; this I could not say. We stood for a while unable or unwilling to move. It was I who knocked first, and I who received the terrible news.'

Janice Flora Whitcomb was twenty-three years old when she died. An enthusiastic watercolourist (mostly flowers of the hedgerow and portraits of her nieces), she had fought the sickness with a determination that had surprised even those closest to her. She would be married, she said, for that was God's purpose.

She was buried in the graveyard of St Mary the Divine in a simple ceremony conducted by the son of the doctor who, twenty-three years previously, had seen her into the world. Present were colleagues and friends numbering over one hundred. Of that number, all but Jem and Pooley stayed to the end, when invited back to the family home.

'You'll have to take care of me now,' Pooley said to Jem.

Unnoticed by a soul they slipped away, disappearing like spirits in the sun-dappled trees.

13

EVEN PEOPLE WHO didn't know him were happy to assert that Mr Frank Dowling, the Editor of *Bell's Life*, knew just about everything and everyone worth knowing. He was also, people said, a fair man, and much was made of the way he highlighted the woeful plight of the poor and downtrodden through the pages of his paper. He was also an acquaintance of Nat Langham, through whom he was both able and encouraged to supplement a fair but modest wage by indulging his passion for gambling. It was this connection also that bought Frank Dowling the honour of being appointed Holder of the Stakes for the upcoming fight between Jem Mace and Madden. As Holder, one of his duties was to appoint the referee, which he did in the shape of a man called Dan Dismore. Dan Dismore was a man so disliked by Nat Langham that, when the hour of the fight arrived and the latter spied the former, an unscheduled fist-fight ensued, which concluded with the Dismore chin being broken and the fight, due to the imminent arrival of the police, being abandoned. It was a ludicrous business and would have signified little had relations between Frank Dowling and Nat Langham not become suddenly so soured that the following Saturday the pages of *Bell's Life* declared for all to read that Mace, for reasons of cowardice had, by refusing to fight, forfeited the match and so given up to the supporters of his opponent the profits from any bets placed.

That night, when the two Beeston boys returned after a long night's walk, to their room upstairs in the tavern on Holborn Hill, it was to find the place shut up, the doors locked. Jem banged on the door. He stepped back. There was a single light burning at a high-up window. He threw a stone hard, heard it clatter against the glass.

The window opened. 'Hey, what's going on?' said a voice thick with sleep.

'Open the door will you?'

'Jem?'

'We're locked out.'

'What are you doing?'

'Freezing our balls off,' said Pooley.

'Where've you been?'

'Just open the door, will you?'

It was good to get out of the cold and to kneel before the embers of a fire.

'So where did you go?' said Robert.

'I don't know,' said Pooley. He looked at Jem.

'Just around. The river.'

'You know Nat was looking for you.'

'Is he here?'

Robert shook his head. 'He came to tell you about tomorrow.'

'Tomorrow?' Jem was warming the palms of his hands before the coals. He turned. Robert was looking awkward. 'What is it? What's happening tomorrow?'

'The re-match. Madden.'

'Tomorrow?'

'Yes...'

Jem stood. His face was warm from the fire. 'So soon? Thank God.'

'What is it?' said Pooley. It was clear there was something Robert Elke hadn't told them.

'Nothing.'

'What is it?' said Jem. 'Is there something wrong?'

'No...'

'Which means there is.'

Robert paused, and took a breath. 'Madden and his people are putting it about that you left the ring first—'

'What?'

'And that you were never intending to fight. He's saying it was all just a set-up. It seems someone stole the purse, and he's saying it was Mr Langham.'

'And does anyone believe it?'

Robert shrugged.

'What does *that* mean?' said Pooley.

'It means not everyone does.'

'But some do,' said Jem.

Pooley shook his head. 'How do you know?'

'Because they were here.'

'Who?'

'I don't know. But they weren't happy. They were saying things—'

'About Jem?'

'And Mr Langham.'

'What were they saying?' said Jem.

'Just foolish things. They'd been drinking.'

'What were they saying?'

Robert sighed. 'Look—'

'What were they saying?'

'That you were a coward.'

Coward.

The word filled the room like a terrible smell.

'When did they go?' said Jem.

Robert shrugged. 'Maybe half an hour ago. Maybe an hour. I don't know.'

'What are we going to do?' said Pooley.

'Wait for the re-match,' said Robert.

'Jem?'

But Jem wasn't listening.

'Jem?'

'I have to go out,' he said.

'Go where?'

He crossed the room, brushing Pooley off.

'You should rest,' said Robert, though he knew such a thing would never happen. He knew that when a man is set on his own destruction no other man can stop him.

'Let him go,' he said to Pooley. 'He'll not find what he's looking for. And then he'll come home.'

'How do you know?'

But Robert Elke said nothing. He wasn't a betting man but had he been he'd have put a shilling and no more on the young man from Norfolk surviving the dark London night and all its terrible demons.

———•——•———

The night and all its demons.

If a plan can have a title then this, it occurs to me, would be mine. I close the *Notes* and consider it. It sounds like the title of a murder mystery, and all the better for that.

It's only a plan of course and, realistically speaking, it is likely to stay that way. Now, with dinner bubbling away on the stove, music on, the wine already open and my son asleep upstairs, one should think of lighter things – things altogether more positive.

Like Mr Fox.

I noted this morning with some satisfaction that the bowl had been licked clean. This I find immensely pleasing, so positively does it underline my role as provider. For someone who, as a young man, was considered unlikely to amount to a thing, this is quite a turn-around and one I would like to share. For the moment, though, providing must be purely its own reward.

———•——•———

Where he went and what he drank not even he could later remember. Whatever he did and whatever he drank, when he woke he was lying in an alleyway, his coat up over his head and an empty bottle by his side. It was after ten in the morning – which would have signified little had it not been for the fact that the re-match with Mike Madden had been set for nine.

With his head pounding he made his way out into the street but couldn't find his way, and when another hour had passed and the alcohol-sweat was streaming off him and the pains in his gut were getting worse, he knew for absolute certain what he needed was a drink. And so he drank. He drank all morning and into the after-noon, and when Mr Harvey of the King's Arms in Bayswater tossed him out, he walked and kept on walking and would have walked right passed the Italianate splendour of Lord's cricket ground, had a group of young gentlemen not recognized his face and led him with the promise of more booze through the gates and onto the manicured grounds. All was going well then until one of the gentlemen – himself the worse for drink – demanded from Jem the return of the fifty pounds he'd wagered and lost the night before – wagered he said on so obvious a coward.

'For a moment,' Jem said, 'I thought my ears had deceived me and that the drink I had so liberally been consuming was confusing all sense. But then my accuser repeated his words, so convincing me they were real. What happened then I will never be able to think of without feeling a terrible remorse. I brought shame not only upon my profession but also my family. It is something that will stay with me until the day that I die.'

What happened was firstly that 'a man of aristocratic birth lost the majority of his teeth and the use of one arm' and, secondly, that the match in progress between William Clark and his All-England Eleven against a team from the United States had to be abandoned, due to the fight spilling on to the pitch and dragging in several members of the opposing team. It was a disgrace, the news of which travelled far and fast. *The Times* declared the affair 'an outrage', while Frank Dowling in the pages of *Bell's Life* referred to Jem as an 'arrant cur' and the 'most unmitigated coward and imposter that ever laid claim to the title of a fighting man'. In conclusion he wrote, 'Every patron of the ring is so disgusted at Mace's conduct that there is happily no chance of his ever again appearing in the fistic arena.'

He was finished.

His career in the ring was over.

But that wasn't all.

There was also the matter of the fire set that night at the door of a labourer's cottage in a small Norfolk village. The woman who lived there – Ann Mace – half roused at the smell of smoke, turned in her bed and opened her eyes. It was midnight but the window was light, sparks flying this way and that. There were voices outside – some she recognized, many she did not. She pushed herself up. Smoke was gathering at the ceiling and catching in her throat as she tried to call out.

No-one was hurt in the fire and little damage done. Except to a family come from gypsies, the bones of whose ancestors had been a part of the land that supported them. But a gypsy is a gypsy and people don't forgive.

When morning came to Beeston it was cold and grey and everything was the same but different too. People gathered at the cottage, some shaking their heads, others stopping to offer a helping hand. Others, though, looked away, and she knew there was talk. During a visit to a smithy in Longdon, her second son, John, had heard the gossips at work – how Jem had defaulted on a fight in London, then failed to turn up for the re-match. It was a disgrace, people were saying, and many were calling him a coward.

She knew how this would hurt him and later, as she stood at the upstairs window of her scarred cottage with her husband and his shallow breathing behind her, she tried to imagine where he was and longed to reach out to him and hold him – but that wasn't going to happen. According to the gossips her boy had disappeared in disgrace. Some had him sailing to America as a stowaway, while others had him dead, the victim of a gambler's revenge. Some claimed he had certainly taken a new name and was working in a Manchester mill; others that he was hiding in his mother's upstairs room.

She squinted hard at the fields and the line of trees far beyond. She tried to make out his shape amongst the shapes of the trees but could not, for not even the keenest of eyes could have seen him from there, as he lay on his back on a deserted piece of scrubland beside the grey, swelling Thames, the scavenging gulls wheeling and cackling above him, the rain beating hard on his flesh and soaking the scraps of his remaining clothes. A bloodied metal pipe lay a few yards to his side.

It took Pooley all night to find him and what he found when he did was a man he barely recognized. Jem was sitting propped up against a wall, his face bloody and swollen, his ripped clothes exposing his pale and bruised body.

'Jem, we have to go.'

He turned his head. 'No.'

'We have to get you cleaned up.'

'Leave me be.' The words came out as a whisper.

'I can't.' Pooley took his cousin's arm. Jem pulled it away, wincing.

'Leave me.'

It was clearly no use talking, so despite Jem's objections, Pooley just pulled him up, wrapping his arm around his cousin's shoulder. Half dragging and half supporting him, he somehow drew them both back to the city's busy streets.

They could hear the club from around the corner, the gentlemen drinkers with their foul breath and braying voices, the scraping of chairs, the cheers for another man beaten to the canvas.

'No,' said Jem.

'Yes,' said Pooley. 'You are owed and this is where we collect.'

Jem shook his head. He could hardly stand.

'Let them see what they did. Let those gentlemen look away when they see who they called a coward.'

No-one seemed to notice when the two men slipped inside. Jem stood back, wrapped in shadows against the wall.

The place was the same – the same foul air blue with smoke, the same smell of cologne and whiskey and genteel corruption. In the ring two men were circling each other like bears in a cage, their hands raised high and their white bodies shining with sweat.

'Wait here,' said Pooley. He paused a moment then pushed his way toward the ring.

'What do you want?'

'To talk about a friend.'

It was hard to hear above the crowd.

'*What* friend?'

'You know.'

Robert Elke squinted across the room. A man was standing in the shadows by the door. As if at some unseen signal he stepped forward, his battered face suddenly lit by the flickering gaslight.

'Good God what's *he* doing here?' said Robert.

'Come to collect what Nat owes him.'

'You can't do this.'

'Announce him.'

'What?'

'Now.'

'I can't.'

'Why not?'

'Instructions.'

'From Langham?'

Robert nodded. 'You don't understand,' he said. Mace was never, he'd been told, to be allowed on the premises.

'Shall I go the magistrate?'

'What?'

'Tell them about Langham's little schemes?'

'You can't do that.'

'Can't I?'

'You don't know him. He'll have you killed. Both of you.'

'Just do it.'

For a moment Robert said nothing. Then, with the deep anguished sigh of a man on his way to the gallows, stepped into the ring and held up his hands. The two fighters paused, turning around to find the source of the sudden quiet.

'Ladies and gentlemen,' Robert said. He glanced at Jem as he dipped beneath the rope. 'Ladies and gentlemen, let me introduce to you someone you should know, a man to whom we all owe our deepest apology...'

Nat Langham heard the commotion from his office. All morning and well into the afternoon he'd been sitting in his office, his head raised up in his most imperious pose at the bidding of Sergei Borruchuk the famous painter.

'What the hell's going on out there?' Nat turned his head.

The painter clucked. 'Still *please*,' he said.

But Nat replied, 'This can wait,' and, flinging the door open, he left the room.

The ring had been abandoned by the current Champion and occupied in his place by a man with his arms held aloft like he was the Champion and not just some drink-sodden has-been. And to make things worse, Robert Elke was standing beside him, addressing the crowd.

'So,' he was saying, 'if this man's not a champion – and I mean a *real* Champion – by the time I make sixty—'

'Hey, you could at least give a fellow a month or two,' a voice cut in, to much laughter and cheering.

'Then my name's not Elke—'

'Hey...'

Robert turned. At once his voice dropped.

Nat Langham was standing there smiling that hard twisted smile of his. 'Could you spare me a minute?' he said. He glanced at Jem. 'Ah,' he said. 'I see the wanderer has returned. And it appears a little the worse for wear. Still, good to be alive, is it not?'

Jem said nothing. He watched the man turn and walk away and the door to his office open and quietly close.

14

OF COURSE MURDER was never a possibility. I have spent some time on this question and have come regrettably to the conclusion that, despite the ease of removing a few cables, I just don't have what it takes. I know I would get caught and, having no wish to go to prison, this is enough to stop me. Besides, the job will be done anyway soon. My sister was told it was a matter of weeks, which, to be honest, was rather more than I'd hoped. Still, overall I can't complain.

Perhaps I should be concerned that, given the imminent death of my father, the slow collapse of my marriage, not to mention my son's injury, the event that has taken up the greater proportion of my thinking-time has been the arrival of my fox, and the seemingly great success of my feeding regime. I fear this either makes me shallow or unbalanced, but feel also that, given the same set of circumstances, who on earth could blame me?

But on to lighter matters.

It occurred to me yesterday, while I was bathing the boy, that in the event of divorce, such an event would become a rarity – if indeed it ever happened again. Whilst this of course would distress me, I do feel I could live with its absence. Which again makes me shallow. Except for the fact that, as a son myself, I know I would have been grateful for my father's absence at bath-time.

But onward. It seems another solitary evening is on the cards. Solitary except of course for the *Notes*. Without them I do sometimes wonder what I'd do.

So, this evening, to the deal.

Jem would fight whenever required at Langham's 'Boxing Saloon' upstairs at The Mitre public house, in St Martin's Lane, in return for his employer's best efforts to rehabilitate his damaged reputation.

But first, by way of sealing the deal, Nat Langham had a surprise in store. Before the young man started work at The Mitre, he would pit him against by far the best fighter he'd ever seen.

Compared with the Rum-Pum-Pas, The Mitre was distinctly second class. There was an earthiness about it that appealed to the rougher end of society. It drew its custom from the slums of the burgeoning East End, and so every night the thick air was filled with the voices of Poles and Hungarians, of Irishmen and Jews, and the men, when they rose to challenge the Champion, were as strong as oxen – so strong in fact, and determined, that in one famous week there were seven new Champions.

'You don't have to do this,' Pooley said.

'Yes I do,' Jem replied.

They were standing – Jem, Pooley and Robert Elke – at The Mitre's paint-chipped door. It was nearly midnight. The place was dark. Jem pushed on the door and went in. He made his way upstairs.

'So you made it then. I wasn't sure you'd come.' Nat Langham was standing in one corner of the ring, dressed for the bout in a pair of long shorts. He'd a belly on him and, though his once formidable frame had shrunk somewhat, there was still something of the fighter about him.

'You?' said Jem.

'Me,' said Nat.

'I thought you'd retired.'

He smiled. 'Call this my final appearance.' The scar on his face bunched and twisted. 'Well?'

Jem turned to Pooley. 'So what do you think?'

'I say do it.'

Robert Elke was shaking his head.

'What's the matter with you?' said Nat.

'Nothing,' he said. The whole thing seemed like madness. He turned away and left the room.

For a man to take such a beating and still be standing after an hour of it has passed and the blows keep coming, means he's either a man who feels no pain or one who feels the pain but doesn't care. Indeed the kind of punishment that would have killed most men Nat Langham received willingly – as if it were a debt he was owed and grateful to collect. When Jem called out, 'Enough?', he just stretched his lips in a bloody grin and forced his body forward. He was a madman or a fool heading into the eye of a storm.

In the end, Jem had no choice but to concede. If he didn't he knew the other man wouldn't stop until he was dead. So he stepped back and raised his hands. The blood ran over his knuckles and down his forearms.

'You did it,' said Pooley.

'You conceding?' said Nat, his voice a defiant whisper.

Jem said nothing.

'Of course not,' said Pooley. 'He damn near killed you.'

'That he did,' hissed Nat.

'So?'

'So what?'

'So you owe him.'

'I believe we had a deal. Didn't we have a deal, Jem?'

Jem looked up. His left eye was closing. He nodded. 'We had a deal,' he said. He was suddenly so tired and all he wanted in that moment were his mother's healing hands and her voice in his ear telling him in a whisper that there was nothing in the world he couldn't do, that no living thing that could stand in his way.

'Jem?'

But when, once and only recently, he'd been able to conjure them – those hands, that voice – now he could not. They would not come. 'Just leave me be, will you?' he said.

'Are you all right?' said Pooley.

Jem said yes, he was all right. Across the ring, Nat Langham was leaning, eyes closed against the rope. 'So much for the noble art,' he said. He paused, slowly opened his eyes as best he could. 'Hey Jem,' he said. 'Do you know what you'll do with the money?'

'What money?'

'When they make you World Champion.'

Jem shook his head. The weariness within him seemed suddenly to have aged him. He felt like an old man. 'I've had enough,' he said.

'Enough?'

'I'm going home.'

Nat Langham nodded. 'Of course you are,' he said.

But he didn't go home and, when he woke the next day, it was to the news that his father had been dead for three weeks, and had been buried in Beeston at St Mary's church on top of the hill.

PART TWO

The Golden Road of
the World

15

THEY RAN AND ran for as long as they could breathe, dipping and weaving through the low-hanging moss, the moist Alabama air thick with bugs, both men filled with thoughts of what was to come.

Three days.

Pooley tumbled, Jem tripped and tumbled too. They lay on the wet ground looking up through the thick jungle canopy, laughing.

Three days.

'Will we do it?' said Pooley after a while, still out of breath.

Jem said nothing. Slowly the laughter subsided. The sun slowly slid in the pale southern sky, the clicks and whirrs of the bayou night rising in response.

For seven weeks they'd been living in a pine wooden shack a mile or so west of the town of Magnolia. For seven weeks, in secret, they'd been running and boxing, their presence unknown to Tom Allen and his boys in New Orleans. Tom Allen and his boys had him already beaten – everyone said so. Mr Sense in the *Times Picayune* said he would sleep with his wife if the Englishman won, everyone else's if he doesn't. A dollar on Mace was a dollar wasted. *Champion of the World?* I don't think so, people said. An old man, they said, a gypsy. Let's send the fellow home in a box.

Pooley laid himself down on the cabin's cool floor. Sometimes at night when he couldn't sleep he would think of the old Cutter barn and how far they'd come. He would think of Nat Langham and Heenan and Brettle, and how each man was the last man, and how each time the cost to Jem was greater, and how nobody but him could see the slow death that was coming. He would think of Beeston and two boys running, and aboard the *Endeavour* on the great Norfolk Wash. He would think of the Rum-Pum-Pas Club and the day

Oscar Wilde came to call. He would lie awake, his heart thumping, strangely fearful.

Jem slumped down on the thick wooden bench, dropping his head between his knees. He looked up. 'I've been thinking,' he said.

'About what?'

'Australia. I've been thinking we should go. When this is all over.'

Pooley sighed and laid his head back down. 'When this is all over,' he said, 'and you're Champion of the whole World, why would you want to go to Australia?'

'I'd like to see the kangaroos.'

'Right,' said Pooley.

'And maybe New Zealand. When this is over.'

A knock on the door. Pooley sat up. 'Who's there?' he asked.

From beyond the door: 'A gentleman to see you.'

Pooley looked at Jem. Jem shrugged.

'All right,' said Pooley. He pushed himself up as Jem slipped into the back room. He crossed the bare wooden floor and opened the door.

It was Johnson from the Magnolia Tree Restaurant. He was turning his hat around in his hands, his black skin shiny with sweat.

'Yes?'

'Like I say,' said Johnson, glancing to his right, 'a gentleman…'

The man was of ordinary height, his hair long and blond, his uniform that of a Union Major General.

'Who are you?' asked Pooley.

The man stepped forward and whipped off his pale calfskin glove. 'Custer,' he said. 'Major General. Pleased to make your acquaintance.'

Pooley took his hand and shook it. The man was unknown to him, his famous name meant nothing.

'May I come in?' said the soldier, and this he did, just as the last of the afternoon gave up exhausted in the face of night's swirling embrace.

———◆———

According to the *Notes*, Jem's meeting with Custer is a legend and is annotated as such. Also so annotated is the 'fact' that the General, who would die a hero six years later at The Little Big Horn, was present at the Allen fight. Whether either is true is impossible to say (Custer was in the area at the time teaching blind children to ride and is known to have followed the world of fistiana). Either way it now scarcely matters except as an indication of my father's willingness to scoot around the truth and then cover himself with an absolving *mea culpa*.

On the subject of which, I can't help wondering how long it will be before he comes clean about my 'mother', who, it seems, has been stalking the wards and is known to all the staff and much liked by them – the same staff, who, on hearing my repeated assertion that my mother died a decade ago, have begun to think of me in a less than positive light. This is a situation that cannot be allowed to go on and will – I am determined on this – be resolved during the course of this afternoon's visit.

But I am moving ahead too fast. If the narrative is to make any sense, Jem has to be got from his deal with Nat Langham and the death of his father to the bayous of Louisiana and the fight that would change things forever.

So.

The death of his father.

—————

It released him from duty but cursed him with the guilt of absence for the rest of his life. Every night when he stepped into the ring upstairs at The Mitre, it was plainly no longer for the glory of it but because hitting and being hit was the only way to numb himself from the pain of failing dreams. Indeed, people said he fought wildly like a man in prison who'd no chance of release – like someone who cares nothing for those around him and even less for himself. No-one – neither Pooley nor Robert – could get through to him.

He was alone one afternoon in his room when he heard a voice calling up from the street. He turned his head on his pillow. His head was pounding from last night – from the fight and the drink that followed – and too heavy to raise. Instead he just turned it on his pillow and stared hard at the wall.

'Hello? Are you there?'

He closed his eyes. Invariably his days were spent holed up in his room and only when Pooley came back from his job at the market stinking of fish did he rise.

They spoke barely a word. For a while, Pooley had tried to persuade him to up and leave, but receiving always the same answer had eventually given up. 'Well *I'm* going,' he'd say – but so far it had only been talk.

A knock on the front door then, 'I know you're there, Mace, and I know you'll want to hear what I have to say...'

Jem opened his eyes.

I know you're there Mace.

Would no-one ever leave him alone? He rose, he fought, he drank, he slept, he fought again. He did his part of the deal – so what if Langham didn't do his? He wasn't complaining. He'd money in his pocket and somewhere to sleep. It was all he needed and all he wanted. That and to be left alone.

'Jem?'

'Go away,' he called out. It took all his breath.

'I will not.'

'Well stay then. But don't wait for me.'

He heard footsteps in the street, then the clatter of a stone against the window. With an almighty effort he pushed himself up, drew back the curtain and opened the window. 'Look,' he said, 'I don't know who you are—'

'You don't?'

'Or what you want. But whatever it is and whoever you are would you just leave me be...'

The voice in the street was that of a pale man dressed in a suit of clothes that must have cost a small fortune. Jem looked a little harder: something about him was familiar. And then it came to him. 'Do you have a son? A small boy?'

'I do,' said the man.

'Then I know you.'

'You do, sir.'

'Wait. I'll be down.'

In the year since he'd visited Jem with his son in the back-room of the Rum-Pum-Pas Club, Lord Drumlarig, eighth Earl of Queensbury, had lost much of his colour and weight. Despite – or perhaps because of – the splendour of his clothes, he seemed more than halfway to death, and a most unlikely opponent, although this was precisely what he wanted.

'I can't fight you,' said Jem.

'Cannot? Or will not? Are you afraid that I'll beat you and send you back where you came from – that Mr Langham and his friends will lose their money to my pocket?'

'Mr Langham? You've spoken to him?'

'I have. And he readily agreed. On one condition.'

'Which was?'

'That in the most unlikely event of your victory I would see to it that you meet Mr Brettle and between you decide who it is has the best claim to being Champion of England.'

For a moment this was too much for Jem to take in. 'Firstly,' he said, 'why would Mr Langham strike such a deal on my behalf? Secondly, I can't fight you – you are plainly ill, and if I punch you I'll kill you and be had up for murder.'

Lord Drumlarig nodded, as if giving the questions much thought. 'Well,' he said, 'firstly, Mr Langham agreed to such a deal because I asked him and he's the sort of man who'd face Bonaparte's army but could never say no to a Lord, and, secondly, while it's true that I may be ill and that one strike from you might end my suffering, then such an outcome is my choice. Rest assured, though, that should such a happy event occur, I shall see to it that the law cannot touch you. Indeed, I shall see to it that your reputation is fully restored as a consequence.' He nodded, in conclusion. 'So what do you say?'

'I don't wish to have a man's death on my conscience.'

Lord Drumlarig cocked his head and smiled. 'But I am already dead,' he said. 'You would merely be lowering the coffin.'

The fight was set for one week hence and although the name of the victor was never in doubt, the manner of his victory would never be known, for his Lordship took a long and solitary walk two days before that date to a glade of outrageous beauty. Here he opened his mouth and placed in it the twin barrels of a shotgun. There followed a report so sudden and so loud that it raised a hundred rooks from the tops of the trees and made a farmer seven fields away turn his head in alarm and start running to the place from where he believed it had come.

16

IT APPEARS THAT my mother is a great lover of thrillers. According to the nurse she brings a new one every couple of days, despite the fact that not a single spine has yet been broken. Were it not for the fact of her grossly insensitive impersonation, I would find this dedication to a lost cause touching. In fact, were she really my mother I would take a great deal of pride in it. But she is not – however much others may believe it.

Anyway, in my absence, circumstances have again gone against me. My father it seems has taken a turn for the worse and the general, though unspoken, consensus seems to be that, despite his looking just about the same as he always looks, the end is near. How near is anybody's guess. Under the circumstances, I didn't feel it appropriate to expose him for the liar he is. There will be plenty of time for that when he's gone.

One interesting thing that emerged from my reading of the *Notes* this morning was that the same source that has General Custer visit Jem in Alabama, also has him, five years later (a year before his death at The Little Big Horn), institute a boxing championship at Fort Bragg in Kansas. The winner of this championship would receive a modest silver cup upon which was engraved the name *Mace – Champion of the World*. While the second does not prove the first, it does perhaps give the story a little more credence. It is a small thing but valuable nonetheless.

In any case, I shall bide my time and continue with the story at hand.

Of course, the death of Lord Drumlarig had repercussions for all those who had once been in his orbit. Naturally, at the termination of his life, his rank and titles alighted on the delicate shoulders of his then sleeping son. So distressed did he become on waking and hearing the news that the memory of that distress would bring a bitterness down upon him, the fingers of which would find the throats of his enemies, one by one – most famously that genius and fool Oscar Wilde.

For Jem, of course, the death meant the end of his chance at a crack at the Champion. The connection had been lost, the chance gone for good.

At least that's what he thought.

But that was to reckon without one of those moments as rare as an eclipse when one man's self-interest matches perfectly that of another – in this case Jem whose career hung entirely on the chance of a bout with the Champion of England, and Nat Langham whose increasingly precarious finances hung likewise on that fight's successful outcome.

The first ever station to be built within the City of London, Fenchurch Street, with its vaulted roof and canopied platforms, was the principal rail link from the capital to the docks at Tilbury and on into the county of Essex and beyond. Visit it now and it is just as it was then...

'Except for those—'

'What?'

Dan Pickering, Chief Stationmaster, points at a man on his cell phone.

'And parking meters,' I say.

He nods. 'And us,' he says brightly. 'Thank goodness.'

'Quite,' I say. 'Just think of the dentistry.'

He shivers. 'Shall we go?'

Upon leaving their cabs in Fenchurch Place, those heading out to the battle of Gypsy and Champion took their seats in the first class carriages (the train would have left from Platform Three), as nervous and excited as new boys on the first day of school. They spoke in hushed voices as the trains pulled away, fearing they might be heard by a government spy and roughly ejected from the train. They giggled at the thought of their wickedness and the prospect of what was to come. They'd be there at a fight to remember, they were sure. Many drank and some snoozed as the train rattled on.

That morning neither fighter knew the whereabouts of the other – that the other was just a carriage away, each accompanied by a group of his own men. The Champion of course had a greater following – the loyal and the shallow and the 'two-way men', who had money on both fighters and so couldn't lose. Jem had Pooley and Robert Elke and a few others, most of whom he didn't know.

One of those in his group went by the name of Simon, though her stage-name was Delilah The Extraordinary Bearded Lady. How she'd come to be there no-one was sure, but she was such good company that no-one objected.

Located on the north side of the Thames estuary, forty miles east of London, Southend-on-Sea had been a fishing village for over two hundred years and would have remained so, had King George IV not decided that his wife would benefit greatly from taking the Eastern waters, the location for which was the village of Southend. Fashion followed the monarch, bringing with it money and status, until there was no better place to hold the Championship of England – a bout still nominally illegal.

From the station, those with tickets for the fight made their way to the wharfside in a fleet of cabs, then by tugboat and steamer across the mouth of the Medway River, and upstream to a small grass-covered, reed-fringed island. Here they disembarked – a number eventually totalling more than five hundred – to join the less well-heeled, who'd made their own way aboard altogether less seaworthy craft.

By eight o'clock the land around the makeshift ring was packed with men and some women enjoying the day's early warmth. There were picnics and laughter, and booze and the usual thievery; while some just lay in the sun, others took exception to overheard remarks and challenges were made. Eight-fifteen passed, then eight-thirty. Nine o'clock came. It was time.

The two fighters made their way through the crowds, who rose to their feet as they appeared, each man the still centre of a whirlwind of cheering and abuse. Though he'd told himself he'd not look, Jem couldn't take his eyes off his opponent, Sam Hurst. Old the Champion may have been, but not in any way that mattered. His muscles were hard, his torso gleaming as if made from beaten bronze. His immense arms were thick and sinewy, his fists as big as cannonballs and black from a lifetime of being toughened with vinegar.

The man was colossal.

Immense.

Unbeatable.

'You see,' said Pooley. 'Old.'

'Then *you* fight him,' said Jem.

'Enough,' said Robert. 'There's work to do here that won't get done with talking.' He eased Jem onto his stool, then turned and, as ritual demanded, threw a glove into the centre of the ring – an act matched by the Champion's man.

Robert turned back and drew in close. 'Jem,' he whispered. 'Remember this. What you do now will change your life and the lives of all that come after you. My father, they'll say, was the Champion. Or my grandfather, and so on, until a century from now some other young man will step into a ring or walk down the aisle or hold his own son in his arms, surer of himself because of you – because of today and what will come of it. Now go out there and do it. You deserve it. It's yours. Take it.'

From the centre of the ring a voice called, 'Time.'

Jem stepped forward in the warm air and he raised his fists and took another step and another, all the time staring at the great bear of a man before him. He suddenly felt so small and so terribly weary, and he longed in that moment for his mother's embrace and the warmth of his father's feet supporting him as he stood to take a piss in the falling snow. He was eight maybe nine and his father's hands were huge and heavy on his shoulders and when he was done his father lifted him up and twirled him around in the snow. Someone was squealing and it was him. There was a pain in his foot that felt like a knife – the Champion had hidden a spike in his boot – and when Jem looked down his own boot was red with blood and the canvas too. When he looked up the Champion was smiling and he thought, *I've lost before I've begun*, and all he could hear was the crowd around him baying for blood, and the pain was rising through his leg so badly that he just wanted to lay down, but something wouldn't let him and instead pushed him forward, and now Hurst wasn't smiling. *What's happening*, he looked like he was thinking, and then Jem felt a blow to his stomach and another that forced the air from his lungs, and he was falling nearly but not quite and the vomit was rising inside him, and he was slipping on the sweat and the blood and the vomit but still standing somehow and in his rage he grew accustomed to the pain. And though Hurst kept coming, his huge fists flying, by the end of the sixth the big man was nearly blind, his face and chest and hands covered with blood and so exhausted he could hardly stand. And though all around were shouting, *Go down Sam for the love of God go down*, he wouldn't go down because who will stand next to the beaten man on a warm springtime street when he's stripped of everything? And so he went on and on, howling, and when at last he fell and his head hit the canvas and a pale-faced man with the narrow face of a greyhound leaned over him and spat in his face – *You stupid bastard!* – he knew it was over, but something hauled him up again and he reached for the man he could no longer see his great hands swinging but then he was down again – *Oh God* – and this time for good...

And the next thing Hurst knew he was sitting on the top deck of a tram in the rain, and he was a dozen years younger, then twenty, and he felt his mother's hands on his face again, rough from the workhouse, and then she was young again and her husband was once again *the most handsome man in the whole of the north*, and they were holding a baby – *We're calling him Sam because the Lord has answered our prayers* – and he's a child again, the shadows on the wall in the upstairs room are faces and trees again, and the night sky such a dark blue, almost black, and he tries to stay awake but he can't stay awake and then it is morning and the start of another day.

'What's the matter, Jem?'

Jem looked down at what was left of Sam Hurst. It was wonderful and terrible and what he knew would be left of *him* one day – what in the end is left of every fighter.

'Jem...'

But then

'Jem, *you did it...*'

then he was riding like a king around the ring, his arms aloft and his head thrown back, and the part of him that was a different part was whispering in his ear that of course he'd live forever and that no-one now could touch him and God help them all if they tried.

17

CREMORNE PLEASURE GARDENS had much in those days to recommend it – especially to those like Jem and Pooley, for whom London was still an unending source of intrigue and amazement. Stroll down the King's Road and through the ornate main gates you'd find cafés and grand oaks, a platform for dancing and a funfair – and, every Sunday, the ascent of a gas-filled balloon. There were musical bands and firework displays, gentlemen's banquets and the exploits of Willie Beckwith, the 'Beckwith Frog', who, every Saturday night, would dress in tie and tails, slip into a ten-foot-high tank filled with water and eat a seven course dinner, finished off with a brandy and cigar. It was the kind of place, during daylight, where children and their mothers would stroll along winding paths buying ice-cream for a penny, while their husbands and fathers made the money that paid for the outing.

Such was the place during daylight.

After dark, however, those husbands and fathers would take their own turns along the blue-shadowed paths, while their children were tucked up in bed at home and their wives squinted hard, as they mended the clothes that made the making of money possible. It was a dual world of innocence and vice, and one in which a single man with money and no father to guide him could mislay what was best in himself and never once mourn its loss. There were whores for a Champion who'd give themselves away for the story they could tell, and even for Pooley, crying for a wife he'd barely known.

She was an American Jew, a half-negro. Her name was Adah Mencken.

'She wasn't *born* a Jew. She *married* a Jew.'

'But she was still a Jew.'

'A *half*-Jew. Like she was a *half*-negro.'

'You can't *be* a half-Jew.'

She'd had three husbands. One of them being John Heenan, Heavyweight Champion of the World.

'You want to hear a joke?'

'Is that a half joke or a whole joke?'

'Yes or no?'

'Okay. The joke. Then can you show me the place?'

'Okay. *So*. There's this first guy who says, "You know, Moshe, if I were as rich as Donald Trump I'd be richer than Donald Trump." "How do you figure that, Heshie?" says the second guy, and the first guy says—'

A cab misses us by an inch. David Leiber, comedian and expert on the history of New York theatre throws his styrofoam cup at the departing vehicle. *Sonofabitch*. We're halfway across 52nd Street heading south. We walk on. He goes quiet. Then he says, 'Did you know she's buried twenty yards from Jim Morrison?'

Yes, I say, Père Lachaise. Last seen on a cold winter's day – around the last time my mother was really free of the pain. 'Did you know,' I say, 'he knew Oscar Wilde?'

David shrugs.

'And Dickens.'

He looks up distracted. 'He knew Dickens?'

'They fell out over Adah.'

'Why?'

'He was jealous of Jem when it was Pooley she really wanted.'

He stops abruptly. He's pointing across the street. 'There it is,' he says. 'The Crown Theatre.'

These days it's a down-at-heel discount store – cheap fabric seconds, plastic sieves, i-Pod covers (two for a dollar). Beyond that there's not much to see – and certainly nothing remaining of those extraordinary times.

'I *told* you,' he says. He shrugs. 'Hey you want a latte?'

I've been walking round the streets of New York for three days now in search of anything connected with Jem. But so far it's as if he'd never been here. All that's left now is an apartment and a bar –

neither of which I can be sure still exist.

'So,' says David. 'What now?'

I tell him my intention to carry on looking.

'And after that,' he says. 'What then? Head back to Liverpool and dig up the corpse?'

I look at him and he's smiling, but there's an edge to it.

'I think they'll have security,' I say.

'You ever think about writing about the living?' he says.

'There's my father,' I say.

'Dead.'

'And me.'

He shrugs, sips his macchiato. 'You know what you should write about?' he says. 'You should write about a man who's father was a shit but it didn't matter. Someone who just says to hell with it and gets on with it. Gets married. Has a kid. Is happy. Oh and by the way. I'd do a little writing on the side.'

'What?'

'The punchline. The two Jews and the one who'd be richer than Donald Trump and so on.'

Outside on the corner the *Don't Walk* sign clicked to *Walk*.

'I have to go,' he says. He seems distracted.

'Are you okay?' I say.

He's fine, he says. That he isn't I only learn later. We shake hands and arrange to meet tomorrow. We part on the corner. I watch him go until he is gone.

She'd had three husbands and scores of lovers. She was an actress at a time when people thought of an actress as little better than a whore – a view much confirmed by her performance in 'Mazeppa' at Astley's Amphitheatre, which was the most shocking event the London stage had ever seen. *A real horse*, people said, *and she rides the thing naked from one side of the stage to the other.* That the horse was indeed real but the nakedness was not mattered little. Women swooned with disgusted delight at the thought of it and men shuffled awkwardly in their seats while rearranging their clothes, before rising at the final curtain to demand something be done to prevent others suffering such an outrage. And it *was* an outrage and so in London, as in New York, the tickets kept on selling and, if you fancied yourself as someone important and you hadn't been outraged, then you clearly weren't important at all. Tickets changed hands in alleyways at hugely inflated prices.

It was scandal and London just loved it.

They met on 4th July 1863 in her dressing-room at Astley's Amphitheatre. Only fame or wealth got you in – and even then you had to wait while the previous entrant's business was concluded. It was sex, people knew, that was going on inside, though of course they never said it, and any man – gentleman or otherwise – who qualified, through rank or income, to stand there in the corridor and wait his turn, felt he knew what it was like to stand waiting with Captain Nolan at Balaclava with the promise of glory or death ahead of him.

All of which was, of course, a ludicrous fantasy. The truth was that Adah Mencken was as much a victim of her background as Jem. Like Jem she'd been born with so many strikes against her that survival was itself a triumph.

She was born Adah Bertha Theodore in the City of New Orleans on 15th June 1835. Her mother was a French Creole and her father a negro – a combination that marked her out in those pre-civil-war days as rather less human than her pale-skinned contemporaries, and, consequently, her choices were limited. There were the fields or the streets. Cotton or a whore's life.

Or, of course, the stage.

'So what *were* you expecting – a horse?'

She danced as a child at the French Opera House, the sallowness of her skin disguised by Mrs Barson's Patented Lightening Powder. She wasn't the best but there was something about her that was better than her betters.

'Well you're not exactly what *I* was expecting. I thought you were some sort of Champion.'

'So what *were you* expecting?'

She shrugged. She felt so terribly weary and just like sleeping. But there was always the public to satisfy.

'What's the matter?' said Jem.

'Matter? Who says there's anything the matter?'

'Well isn't there?'

Adah looked straight at the Champion. The Champion looked straight back. There was something in his look that she recognized. 'Don't you ever feel,' she said, 'like just sitting down? I mean just doing nothing—'

'You do nothing and nothing happens,' said Jem.

'Yes, but wouldn't that be nice?'

'You want to sit?'

'I don't mean now.'

'What's wrong with now?'

'But what will people think?'

'They won't know. And anyway, they'll think what they always think – that you're a whore and I'm a gypsy.'

And so they sat – whispering like children on a mountain of cushions while outside in the corridor a line of young Earls and other wealthy men were discretely re-arranging their trousers.

They were friends and remained so, until she and the horse and the show left for Paris. He and Pooley would meet her at the stage door and the three of them would explore the city together. Their friendship was something new for them both, and it was something they knew would endure. They never talked about things that mattered – the war in America, the ever-tightening grip on the fight-game, the fact of Jem's marriage – because everything that mattered to them was in some way implicitly understood. They were like children who'd got away – sneaking out of the poorhouse when the Beadle wasn't looking – and had somehow done more than survive.

But survival, at least, wasn't to endure.

When her fall from the horse happened, it caused barely a ripple in the stalls. *Perhaps she was meant to fall*, people thought, then thought no more of it. But something ruptured inside her.

This was compounded by the drink. She drank and Jem drank and sometimes, when they walked, they staggered. Sometimes, drunk, Jem and Pooley would square up and trade wild, hopeless punches. The man from *The Times* called them 'Animals in a zoo', and explained their behaviour with reference to their parentage and consequent lack of morals and restraint. If Jem had ever told himself, and believed, that a man could make himself in this greatest of Empires, then he knew differently now.

One morning, Adah Mencken took the boat-train to Paris. Jem didn't go to see her off and they never saw each other again. When, many years later, he stood by her graveside in Paris, an onlooker reported that he spoke to her as if she were living and as if he were mad. But they were neither.

18

His wife was a woman of absolutely no importance. Her name was Mary. Her name was Selina. Her name was Hannah. And there were children – a dozen of them – about which he cared little. He was never there. He was on the road, he was on the Wash, he was in the bed of a half-negro actress. They came, were deserted and divorced him. There was casual bigamy and deceit, and there was even a jilting at the altar. They followed him, dragging his unwanted children behind them. He cared little, he said, for the rules of the church – and even less, it seems, for the feelings of the women who adored him.

'So you're saying he was a shit.'

'He was.'

'Were you there when he died?'

'I was in the canteen. Or maybe I wasn't. I don't remember.'

We're in a bar in The Village, David waiting for his sister, me just waiting.

'How did it feel?'

'I don't know.'

'You don't know how it felt?'

'Yes. Like I don't know what being born felt like. I was *there* too.'

As I knew it would this hippy-tinged vagueness seems to satisfy David and he goes back to looking out at the street.

'What does your sister look like?' I say.

'Jewish,' he says.

'And she's an actress.'

He turns, grinning. 'Never rode no horse across no stage though,' he says.

'It's something worth thinking about,' I say, as the hard New York rain starts to fall.

———◆———

The legacy of his wives was guilt and children; the legacy of his dalliance with Adah Mencken, a note of introduction to one of her former husbands, John Heenan. John Heenan was an American, a New Yorker, and had once been the Heavyweight Champion of the World.

I'd be glad to see you, he wrote, *and to spar with you. You are well known here and could make considerable money. The offer stands as long as you do.*

There was just one problem.

And the problem's name was Inspector Gold.

Whether it was due to his having been bullied as a child, or a simple love for the law that propelled Inspector Gold to a career of such doggedness now matters little. *Then,* of course, it mattered a great deal. *Then,* with the newly-formed Police Force out to prove itself, and the law having long since spoken on the matter of bare-knuckle fighting, it was the duty of men such as Inspector Gold to uphold that law and send those involved before the courts to suffer the weight of justice. That this meant a great deal of sneaking around and, in some cases, the adoption of the most unlikely of disguises was immaterial to the intrepid Inspector Gold. He would stand in alleyways and cup his ear to listen; he would cover the palms of informants with silver. His ears would prick up in the snug bars of pubs and his nose would twitch like a lurcher's. If he heard the word Brettle or Stevenson or Mace, his heart would flutter and for months he crept around the dark London streets and was sometimes mistaken for a vagrant. This he didn't mind – for who would care if such a wretch listened in? Indeed, he increasingly donned the rags of a homeless drunk, in order to winkle out intelligence. And, time and time again, such intelligence was forthcoming. Time and time again, he would listen and wait and take notes in a little brown book. Then, weeks and sometimes months later, he would spring (notwithstanding his limp) and, with the assistance of a number of blue-suited bobbies, he'd arrest all present and deliver them like babies into the savage willing arms of a magistrate.

Which was all very well.

But it wasn't enough.

His one greatest failure was not anticipating the championship of England at which Mace the Gypsy had lifted the belt and himself into a life of money and women. That it was partly the absence in his own life of these two fine commodities that drove his special hatred for Mace is clear, but Jem's foul heritage also played a part. Many years ago, Gold had been attacked. His knee had been shattered so comprehensively in the process that it had left him with a life-long limp. He believed his attackers had been gypsies, and it was gypsies who would pay for it – legally, of course, but they would pay.

The first he heard about the Stevenson fight was from a prostitute who'd been with a man called Cramer. He, in turn, had heard it from a man whose brother was a Walthamstow dog-man responsible for sharpening a fighting dog's teeth. Somehow, as a consequence of this unlikely chain, enough information had crept out for the forces of the law to be marshalled.

The date was the most important thing and Inspector Gold had it. Next was the location – Hackney Marshes – and he had that too.

He was ready to go.

The raid (if such a hopelessly confused affair could be so described) took place at nine o'clock in the morning – the hour at which the fight was to begin. Inspector Gold and his colleagues tumbled from their hansom cabs and, running as best they could through the marshy lanes, prepared to do their duty. They raised their truncheons and cleared their throats and found as they rounded a high hedgerow...

Nothing.

The place was deserted.

Inspector Gold had been fooled and everyone knew it. As he searched the horizon, as if tracking the movements of figures others couldn't see, he tried not to feel the pitying looks and tried not to hear the giggles and whispers.

The journey back from the marshes was the most humiliating of his life – so much so that when, at last, the specially-hired train pulled into Fenchurch Street, he abandoned his fellows and made his way straight to the last known address of Jem Mace. It was a modest house in Chelsea (then genuinely a village) owned by an attractive young woman of means, who would, many years hence, lose her life aboard the SS *Titanic*.

Gold knocked on the door with undisguised purpose. He called through the letter-box. He skirted the property and, against all the rules, he let himself in through a poorly-bolted door.

He was halfway up the stairs when he heard the sound of voices. One was a man's, the other clearly that of a woman. Clearly they were not playing cards.

He crept to the door and turned the handle. It was locked.

'Come out!' he called. He stepped back at the sound of whispering. He raised his boot and kicked the door in.

For a moment all was chaos – the rattling of a window, flying bedclothes and cursing. And then he spotted him – the big foreign-looking man, half in, half out of the window. Gold dashed across the room, aware of a woman's hands upon him, from whose grasp it was hard to escape.

'Let me go!' he cried. 'I'm on the Queen's business!' He lunged for the fleeing man's foot but caught only the sole of his boot, which came away in his hands. The man would surely have fled had Gold not made another grab and this time found an ankle, and tugged and tugged and tugged, until he felt the man's resistance lessen, and he felt a sudden thickness of blood between his fingers.

'What's this?' he said.

'You've killed him!' screamed the woman hysterically.

'You're under arrest,' said Inspector Gold.

'On what charge?' said Jem.

For a moment the Inspector was stumped. 'Breaking and entering,' he said at last.

'But I was leaving.'

'And suspicion.'

'Of what?'

'That,' said the dogged Inspector, 'is for the Magistrate to decide. Now, will you come quietly, or are you determined to make things worse for yourself?'

Jem slowly made his way back in through the window. He'd cut his thigh on the broken glass of the window and it was bleeding steadily. To the surprise of the Inspector the gypsy's blood was red like his own.

Inspector Gold gripped the man's arm. It was as thick as a tree-trunk. The man was as strong as an ox, but he had the law on his side, and the law was as strong as the very word of God.

The resulting case was confused and ambiguous. While the charges as read pertained to the illegal act of bare-knuckle fighting, these were eclipsed, once evidence of his bigamy was produced (to the delight of those in the public gallery).

Although he spoke well and struck a fine figure, he was clearly a brute at heart – no more or less so than any of his kind. Women in the gallery swooned delightfully when he caught their eye, later speaking of his look as that of a vicious, lustful animal, while many a man in the court wished him dead.

Death, however, the court wasn't at liberty to provide. The best that could be managed was disgrace – to declare him an enemy of the nation. As for the sentence, this remained undecided for a while. In the meantime, Jem Mace, the Champion of England, was free to walk the streets if he dared – free but finished as a fighter.

But fighting was all he had and they knew that. They knew that he was nothing but a jumped-up, stinking gypsy, and that he would sink back into the gutter from whence he had come.

19

As the son of a Jew and the son of a son of a Jew, David Leiber knows as much about the sweet, caressing sharpness of the six-pointed star as any man alive. He also knows a good deal when he sees one. Which was how, at the age of twenty-six, he had the courage to abandon his tedious and spiteful partner and their luxurious north London semi, for the promise of a new life in America.

Within a month of arriving in New York, he was married and had so impressed his superiors in the School of Jewish Studies at City College, that there was already talk of extending his contract.

Come over, he'd say to me, I've something to show you. And, when I could at last, I did.

'Well?'

'Are they real?'

'No, I had them made up special... Of course they're real. Try them on.'

They fit perfectly – *like a glove* you could say.

'Where did you get them?'

'I bought them.'

I turn them over, hardly able to believe I'm wearing the sparring gloves *he* wore – that these are the gloves in which he prepared to fight John Allen.

'Drink?'

I turn them back, slip them off. 'But where did you get them?'

'eBay. And I know what you're thinking. How do I know they're the real thing? Well, you know how many hours your dad and my dad used to spend – waste we used to think – talking about this stuff?

Well, did you ever hear them talk about the ring Adah gave him – the Jewish one with the pointed stone?'

'Of course,' I say.

'Well feel inside.'

And I do and there it is – a worn-away section of the fabric inside, where the point of the ring would have been.

'You know he was wearing it the day he landed.'

'You don't know that for sure.'

'Was my dad ever wrong?'

I have to concede. David's father was the least wrong person I'd ever known. Unlike my father, he'd always seemed to know everything.

So do you want that drink or should we go?'

'Where are we going?'

'To see where he landed.'

'You make it sound like the moon.'

——•◆•——

In late September 1869, the liner *City of Antwerp* landed in New York, having made the voyage from Liverpool in record time. The *Antwerp* was spruce, as befits a ship on only its second outing, its beds well sprung, its rails brightly polished. In command was a man by the name of John Moorhouse, whose loves were the sea, fistiana and his wife, apparently in that order. Hearing that Jem was on board, he summoned him to the bridge and allowed him to steer. In a moment of grim and accidental prophesy he is said to have said, 'Just watch out for icebergs' – something that the next-but-one of his successors later failed to do, as the ship struck an iceberg in the Autumn of 1890, and went down with the loss of forty lives.

John Heenan was at the quayside to meet him. A former Champion of America, Heenan was five years younger than Jem but already retired. Like sportsmen before and since, he'd made enough money to get out and had bought a series of bars, although none of them ever made a single cent. He was broke, but there was still money to be made in staging 'Exhibitions of the Fistic Arts', especially if the man across the ring was the Champion of England.

For Jem, however, this would never be enough. He needed a real fight. He needed Allen.

But for now there was Heenan and his endless talk of Adah and how she'd betrayed him with a dozen or a hundred men. If he knew that Jem was one of them he never said. Either he didn't know or he needed the exhibition money too much to remember. Either way the money came in and went out – often more the latter than the former.

———

'So what did he say?'

'About what?'

We're standing at Ground Zero, squinting in the sunlight through the mesh.

'About this woman – your "mother"?'

Teams of hard-hatted workmen were scouring the pock-marked earth like gulls on the dump at Staten Island.

'I didn't speak to him.'

'Not at all?'

'It was too late.'

'Jesus.'

I shrug.

'Did you *see* her?'

'Yep.'

'And?'

'And she looks like my mother. She looks like *your* mother.'

'So it was just a mistake then. A misunderstanding.'

'Maybe.'

What looks like a mile or more across the site, two men in hard hats are arguing, jabbing their fingers at each other. In a while another man appears and breaks them up.

'So it's not so bad then,' David says.

I say no, not so bad, and I want to say more but don't.

Later that night I'm sitting in my room turning over the pages of the *Notes* when it occurs to me that what I'm seeking is really gone. It's a simple thing but hits me with the full force of truth. Jem has been dead for nearly a century and my father for nearly a year. But there are no degrees of dead. Dead is dead. Dead is gone.

The next morning I find myself riding the subway north-east out to Morris Park in the Bronx and the Golden Trinity Gym. It was here over a hundred years ago that Jem spent so much of his time. Back then the place was just starting up – its immigrant owner, Laurentin O'Dowd, the thirteenth son of a family of Dublin potato farmers, was in need of something or someone to raise the profile of his gym above that of all the others that were springing up around the city in the years immediately after the end of the civil war.

And who better for the job than Jem Mace the Champion of England?

'Yes, sir, can I help you?'

'I've been looking for Jem Mace,' I say.

'Jem *who*?'

I explain the connection. There, in that place, it seems even more distant than usual.

The face of the black man in the door's peephole window creases up in a frown. 'Why the hell're you botherin' me?' he says.

I consider explaining again, but I'm suddenly aware of the distance from where I am to the nearest place of safety. 'I was just hoping I could take a look,' I say instead.

The peephole slams shut. I raise my hand to knock again but something invisible stops me. I wait. And wait.

After maybe ten minutes the peephole slams open. 'You still here?' The man's teeth are the whitest I've ever seen, his skin rich and rippled like the chocolate in a commercial. Again the peephole slams. This time, though, there follows the sound of locks being turned.

Thanks to Jem, this particular boxing speakeasy flourished and, as the generations passed, all kind of people came and went, from the Boston Strongboy John L. Sullivan to future president, Theodore Roosevelt, and Ernest Hemingway, in whose honour the bi-annual 'Papa's Cup' is awarded to the current most promising newcomer.

'So did you ever meet him?' I say.

'How long did you say he's been dead?'

'I meant Hemingway.'

JT Diamond shrugs. 'Sure,' he says.

'So what was he like?'

'Like? Crazy. You know he got hit so hard one day he lost a tooth. He sits up and you know what he says? "The son also rises." He was always so pissed at his daddy. I don't know why.'

'You didn't ask him?'

'Why would I ask him? Ain't my business. Is this what you wanted to see?'

In Jem's day the ring was in the corner of the room, the rest of it busy with all the paraphernalia of boxing and the fighters themselves, with their long shorts and their hungry-looking immigrant faces. They were Irish and Poles and Italians and Jews – men who had come to America to rid themselves of the Old World's decay and to breathe in the clear air of the new.

'You see that?' JT Diamond is pointing to a small square table set discretely in the far corner. It's piled high with papers and several bottles of water. 'You know who sat at that table? Mr *Mu*hammed Ali. 'Course he was Cassius Clay then, and skinny as a polecat. You know he couldn't write his own name until my daddy taught him how? But then he wouldn't stop. Take a look.' Across the room, below the barred window, he points with a stubby finger to a childish scrawl:

cassius clay champion

'You see that?' he says. Yes, I say. For the first time JT Diamond seems every year of his age: suddenly he has about him the childlike quality that often returns to the very old.

'Maybe writing and boxing don't mix,' I say. 'Jem couldn't write. Not a word. Never learned.'

'They were hard times,' says JT.

'He could dance though.'

JT smiles.

'They say if he hadn't been a boxer he would have been a dancer. They say he would have been a star. In fact he *was* a star. He'd walk down Broadway and people would point and stare. "There goes the gypsy from England," they'd say, and he'd smile and wave his cane. He had a top hat too. Did you know he owned a bar?'

'Did he lose it?'

'He lost it.'

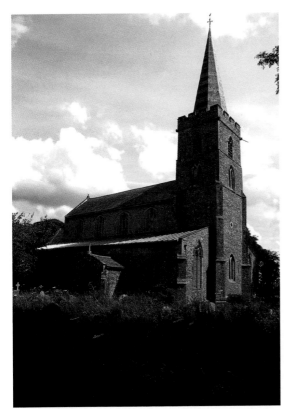

St Mary the Virgin, Beeston, the final resting place of Jem's father, William Mace.

The Ploughshare Inn, Beeston. Only the left-hand wall remains of the original one-room alehouse.

The village of Beeston: the cottage in which Jem was born stood on what are now the allotments in the foreground.

Southend-on-Sea: the fight with Sam Hurst for the Championship of England.

JEM MACE,
CHAMPION OF ENGLAND.

Born at Beeston, Norwich, on Good Friday, April 8, 1831.

Height, 5 feet 9 inches.　　　　Average Weight, 10 Stone 10 Pounds.

PRINCIPAL BATTLES.

Beat SLACK, October 2nd, 1855.
Beat THORPE, February 17th, 1857.
Beaten by BOB BRETTLE, September 21st, 1858.
Beat POSH PRICE, January 25th, 1859.
Beat BOB TRAVERS, February 21-22, 1860.
Beat BOB BRETTLE, September 9-20th, 1860.
Beat SAM HURST, June 13th, 1861.
Beat TOM KING, January 29th, 1862.
Beaten by TOM KING, November 26th, 1862.
Beat JOE GOSS, September 1st, 1863.

Draw JOE COBURN, October 4th, 1864.
Draw JOE GOSS, May 24th, 1866.
Beat JOE GOSS, August 6th, 1866.
Draw NED BALDWIN, October 15th, 1867.
Beat TOM ALLEN (America), May 10th, 1870.
Draw JOE COBURN, America, November 30th, 1871.
Draw NED BALDWIN, July, 1872.
Beat JOE COBURN (America), twice.
Beat BILL DAVIS (America), £1,000, Virginia City.
Beat BILL DAVIS (America), 600 dollars, San Francisco.

Jem's CV.

Pooley, Robert Elk and Jem in New York.

The young Wyatt Earp,
whom Jem befriended.

Adah Mencken at the time of *Mazeppa*.

Charles Dickens, friend of Jem and fellow
late-night walker.

Mace the Dandy.

The New Orleans bronze memorial of the Mace–Allen fight for the Championship of the World.

Mace (right) and Joan Heenan.

Tom Allen and Jem Mace in a publicity still from the big fight. The gloves were for sparring only.

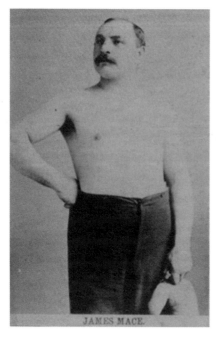

Jem at the time of his Australian tour.

Jem at 78, the year before his death.

Jem's marker on a once unmarked grave.

Jem with his great-grandson,
the author's father.

The door across the room opens. A black boy – fourteen, maybe fifteen years old, in a hoodie – slopes in. The door closes behind him.

He nods at JT and slips off his headphones.

He glances at me.

I smile.

He doesn't. He squeaks across the wooden floor in his trainers and disappears into a back room.

'The next Champion?' I say.

'No, sir,' says JT. 'The next Pope.'

In those days, on Sundays, the ring became a pulpit, from where Jim 'The Fighting Preacher' McGarry would hold forth on the moral turpitude of the modern world, before dispensing with his surplice and revealing his shorts, and his readiness to beat any man to hell and back if he dared take the name of the Good Lord in vain.

He was a big man, but no match for Jem. With Heenan looking on, the Gypsy from England famously knocked The Preacher off his feet and clean out of the ring with a single punch. It was a punch so decisive and so unexpected that, for a moment, there was as close to silence in the Golden Trinity as there had ever been.

It was a punch, the power of which would, in the weeks ahead, spread throughout all the gyms in the city and make Jem Mace the only fighter worth fighting and beating, and one of only two contenders for the undisputed Championship of the World.

20

It NOW SEEMS beyond any reasonable doubt that our friend Mr Fox is dead. For three nights now I have crept downstairs through a quiet house only to wait in vain for his arrival. The bowl of food remains untouched and it seems only a matter of time before I will have to face the fact that this cheering little episode is over. Which is not to place too high a value on the thing – he was after all just a fox. Vermin some would say, though not I. It is, I believe, not unusual for a man who is under a great deal of stress to come to depend on something that would appear to others perfectly trivial. In my case that something is, or was our friend Mr Fox.

However. Such is now the situation. My son, having begun to recover, has also begun to ask a few awkward questions. Why do mummy and daddy no longer sleep in the same room? And why, if everything is fine, is there so much shouting? Both are questions that up to now I have managed to skirt around – though I fear not for much longer. Every day he grows older and more attuned to the lies and deceptions of adulthood.

But that – though close – is still for another day. For now I am both willing and grateful to bury myself in the past. It is after all *my* past too. It is, after all, Jem's blood that flows through my veins. It is, after all, his heritage upon which mine is built, his story which informs and directs my own.

So.

The fight. Tom Allen. The bougainvillea and jasmine of the American south.

CHAPTER TWENTY

According to the *Times Picayune*, in that spring of 1870 New Orleans was experiencing its longest spell of dry weather since before the Civil War. The Mississippi was low and the primitive levees were under no threat – nor, most believed, was the Champion's crown. The Champion was, after all, ten years younger than his opponent, and all believed a decade in the fight game was a lifetime in any other. To many, consequently, it was a mismatch and could only ever have one outcome. This was certainly true in one sense, in that one outcome *was* certain.

The winner would be English.

How strange that they should come *here* – these two Englishmen – to fight for the Championship of the World, and what a strange twist of history that they should fight for it in the city of New Orleans, capital of the slave trade, where so many Englishmen had made their bloody fortunes and so many negroes had finally arrived in what would one day call itself the land of the free – though it was still not that for them then. And how ironic that the city that had been spared the ravages of the Civil War – bypassed by Sherman's brutal 'hurricane march' through Georgia to the sea – should one day be flattened by a hurricane that came from the sea, leaving death and devastation in its wake.

'You lookin' for *what?*'

With much of the Louisiana National Guard on tour of duty in eastern Iraq, those left behind, charged with maintaining law and order, had been stretched from the start and were, in many cases, unable to help those who needed it most or prevent those whose only concern was to steal from their fellow man.

'There's a statue. Two fighters. I was told it was someplace near the airport.'

Janelle – I'm Here To Help! shrugs and glances at her colleague who's busy filling bagels and wrapping them in cellophane. Though it's clear she thinks I'm crazy there's a weariness about her judgment, as if, thanks to her job selling bagels at Louis Armstrong International Airport, she has seen so many crazy people from so many different places that one more barely registers.

'You know about some statue?' she says.

'It's bronze,' I say. 'About so high,' I raise my hand to indicate about seven or eight feet. 'It's a memorial to a famous boxing match in 1870.'

'In *when*?' Janelle's colleague looks up, squinting hard, as if he's trying to see something that is way too far away to be seen.

'1870,' I say. 'But hey, it doesn't matter—'

'Well if it don't matter, why are you botherin' me?'

I say sorry and step away. I know what you mean, something inside me wants to say. In a moment I'm lost once again in the crowds.

The Big Easy had been chosen as the scene of this greatest of fights for two reasons. Firstly, public fighting for money had not yet been made illegal in the State of Louisiana (with the exception of the very centre of the city), as it had in the State of New York and many others. Secondly, the district of New Orleans was considered far enough away from the thugs and hooligans and flourishing crime families of the north-east to make their mass attendance unlikely. Today, implementing such a minor precaution seems bizarre; then, however, crime was still mostly local, and deals were concluded face to face, one man in the presence of another. They were simpler times and brutal with it: when you killed a man, you watched the light leave his eyes as he died.

The news this evening is that we should prepare ourselves for the worst. They don't specify what that worst might be, of course. If they knew, for example, that in my case the worst would be the news that he'll live as long as me, I think they'd be surprised.

But, of course, that's not what they mean and my sister is at least performing the requisite act of foreboding. 'They say it's not long,' she says.

I set my face in a frown. 'But how long?' I want to say – but do not. I couldn't trust myself not to add, 'What? *That* long?' So I keep quiet, safe in the knowledge that the staff on the ward (all but Nurse Bellingham, who, I believe, has got me figured out) will take my silence as evidence of premature mourning, which reflects well both on him as a father, and me as a loving and dutiful son.

21

THE PRIVILEGED SING their joyous songs, while violence stalks the shadows. Thus was the city of New York then, and so is it now. *Then*, when Hannah arrived with Robert Elke and Ada aboard the *City of Paris*, it was a city of mud streets and glittering ballrooms – of fortunes gathered through speculation and men made cripples by war. It was the land of opportunity – the chance to succeed and to fail. For Jem and Pooley, it was by far the wildest place they'd ever seen, a city released from the shackles of war and given up to excess of all kinds. For those who could afford it, there were nightclubs that opened at midnight and only closed when the last man standing had drunk himself into a stupor, and the last of the ladies had found a partner with enough cash to pay for a room in some flop-house in The Bowery, where a man would be waiting with a club and the necessary will to use it. For all but the poorest, New York was a city unattended by conscience – if you had it then you deserved it and if you didn't, well, that's too bad for you. It was the eve of Empire, the American century's first distant stirrings.

Four months previously, and within an hour of the *City of Antwerp* tying up at the dockside, Jem and Pooley had, thanks to Heenan, found themselves in O'Brien's Bar on Broadway, the centre of great speculation. When would he fight, the men wanted to know, and was there a fortune to be made in the fight game? Meanwhile the women looked for evidence of a ring on his finger and, finding none, checked themselves in the mirror that hung over the bar, and showed a little more flesh than they'd planned to show that morning.

For Jem, O'Brien's was a world away from Norwich and Beeston and the Old Cutter Barn. Such was his greeting and the attention he received that he knew in that moment, as O'Brien himself (who ordinarily could barely stand the presence of an Englishman in his bar) raised a cheer in his honour, that he'd never go back and would never have to, and, when within an hour of leaving O'Brien's Bar on Broadway, he and Pooley were climbing the dimly lit stairs of Francesca's Powder Room with its stairwell windows looking onto the dark and seething park, it was clear that when he died, there'd be mourners by the hundred walking slow and weeping behind his coffin, and a statue erected, around which in years to come, all would gather to remember him.

It was *hubris in extremis*, which, by the time the *City of Paris* had arrived four months later, had either changed Jem or revealed his true nature. Either way it made of him a man so conceited and sure of his enduring appeal that Hannah would not have known him, had she not recognized his face. And, had Robert Elke not sat in the drawing room on West 26th Street with three-year-old Ada and seen with his own eyes the disdain with which Jem ordered his *servants* to and fro, he would not have believed it. Nor would he have believed that the shy young man whom he'd met so long ago at the Rum-Pum-Pas Club would ever have been happy to offer himself, stripped to the waist, on a New York stage, as a celebrity 'turn' between acts, during which he would pose as a Greek statue and *then* offer kisses back-stage at fifty cents a time or three for the bargain of a dollar.

'So you're making a good living, then?' Robert asked.

'I have friends,' he said, resenting the intrusion.

And then there was Ada. At three, though she was his daughter, she was a stranger and of absolutely no interest to Jem. She would stand in the corner of a room and watch him as he dressed or watch from the window, as her mother and father and cousin Pooley stepped into a cab with a shiny black horse and were gone.

'These friends,' said Robert. 'What do they want?'

'They want me. They want to be seen with me. They want to be seen with the Champion of England and the next Champion of the World. Don't you?'

'Me?'

'Isn't that why you're here? To be a part of it? A part of *me*?'

Robert shook his head. He sighed and looked down at his knees. 'What does Pooley think?'

CHAPTER TWENTY-ONE

'Pooley? He loves it. And the women love him.'

Robert looked up. 'Because of you.'

'Yes. Because of me.'

'And what about Hannah? Does she want to be a part of it?'

'She is a part of it.'

'Whether she likes it or not.'

Jem shrugged. He crossed to the window. He withdrew a cigar from a box on a stand and lit it.

Behind him, Robert Elke reached forward and lifted a heavy silver belt from the table. 'It's fine work,' he said.

Jem said nothing. He was watching the activity in the street below.

'Shouldn't you have *won* something to get it?'

His shoulders tightened.

'I mean you usually get the belt after the fight. Isn't that right?'

Jem turned. He smiled. 'It was a gift from friends,' he said. 'From Tiffany's. A gift from people who *believe* in me.'

'So you win, they win, right?'

'Right.'

'What if you lose?'

'I won't lose.'

'Everybody loses. In the end.'

'Not me.'

'Even you.' Robert replaced the belt and sat back. 'Did I tell you I saw Sam Hurst? I passed him on the street. Or I would have done if I hadn't recognized him. The smell was terrible. Whiskey and piss. You know he asked after you? Even lying there on the street he asked after you. So I told him where I was going and what you were doing and you know what he said? He said he'd save you a place. Keep it warm. You see he knows you. Better than any man.'

'He doesn't know me.'

Robert nodded. 'He does. He *was* you—'

'He was *never* me.'

'—although he never let himself be owned.'

'You don't know what you're talking about.'

'I'm talking about the friends who gave you that belt. You think they'll ever leave you alone now? You think they'll be happy to let you walk away whether you win or lose? You think you won't owe them still, either way?'

'I win, I'm the king. I can do what I want.'

'You win and you're theirs. You lose and you're nobody's. And you think they'll just say they're sorry and let you walk away?'

Jem turned sharply. 'Look,' he said. 'I paid your ticket and here you are. So what do you want to do? Keep talking like this or help me win?'

Robert said nothing.

'I could pay your ticket home too, if that's what you want. Is that what you want?'

Just then the door opened. It was Pooley. He was clearly drunk. On his arm was a rouged and tipsy woman. Robert stood and looked at Jem.

'Good evening,' said Pooley.

'Goodbye,' said Jem, staring coldly at the woman.

'What?' she said, her heel turning. She looked squinting at Pooley. 'What's he saying?'

'Nothing,' said Pooley. He looked hard and with bitterness at Jem, then at Robert. His face softened. 'He say he'll send you back home yet?'

'It's under discussion,' said Robert.

'Just get her out of here,' said Jem.

Robert rose and crossed the room. 'I'll let you know my decision,' he said. He paused before the woman and pointedly raised his hat.

———◆———

'Excuse me, are you the son?'

...and pointedly raised his hat.

I lift my eyes from the *Notes*. 'Yes,' I say.

'Then could you possibly come with me?'

'What's happened?'

'If you could just come with me.' I glance at the *Notes* – *He smiled at Pooley then turned to the door, opened it and was gone* – then return them to my bag and follow. We walk down a long, yellow corridor hung with patients' feeble watercolours and posters about eye-care, and into another waiting room where I'm invited to sit. There is no-one else in the room except for a small girl sitting alone on a chair.

'Won't be a minute,' the nurse says.

I look at the small girl and smile. The girl looks away. *If a strange man smiles at you*, she's probably thinking, *call the police.*

A strange man.

I catch a glimpse of myself in the re-enforced window. I look ten years older. Nothing like the pictures on our mantle at home.

I sit back and close my eyes. *This must be what waiting for death is like.*

Jem hadn't spoken to Robert for nearly a month when the day came to leave for the south. What is more, despite Pooley's best efforts to persuade him to continue he'd abandoned the training programme and had even quit running. Instead he'd eat and go out on the town, and he seemed not the slightest bit unsettled by either the fast-approaching fight date or his sudden need to purchase a new dinner suit, the old one having grown prohibitively tight. He was a man trading exclusively on what he would become, without tending to the work such an ambition requires.

They gathered beneath the chandeliers at Penn Station – Jem and Pooley and a hundred or so of their newest, closest friends.

'Who are they?' Pooley whispered but Jem didn't or wouldn't hear him.

They were following him and they believed in him and that was all that mattered. Indeed, so many clasped his hand and slapped him on the back and caused such a ruckus that many of those others at the station unconcerned with the fight believed themselves to be in the presence of the President or at least Bob Ferguson of the Brooklyn Atlantics, and they craned their necks to see, only then to move on disappointed. There were others though – those who did know the game and what was at stake – who stood back in the shadows with pale and serious faces and overcoats draped over their arms.

At every station heading south there were people there to see him. They thrust books and papers at him for him to sign, not knowing, of course, that this was something he couldn't do. Instead he waved and smiled and took their good wishes, unaware that it wasn't really *him* they were there for, but anyone who'd take on the Yankee (as

Allen was generally believed to be), and do to him what the Yankees had done to the south.

'So what now?'

'What do you mean, "What now?"'

The train was slowing as it approached New Orleans. Jem had his head out of the window, his eyes squinting in the wind as they searched for first sight of the oncoming station.

'I *mean* what are you planning to do?'

'*Do?*'

'You have to get the weight off. You have to run. You have to think what Robert would say.'

'Robert?'

'And just hope he comes.'

Jem pulled his head in. His face was flushed from the wind, his hair wild. 'I don't need him,' he said. He looked like a little boy.

'You need him,' said Pooley, as the train slowed and the brakes hissed and squealed, and they pulled slowly into the chaos and heavy midday heat of the station.

Shelby Cobb was a black man who'd lost count of his age around seventy. He'd been a slave in the cotton fields and would have carried a musket for the south if they'd allowed him, instead of working until his back was nearly broken and waiting for the Yankees to come set him free. And come they had, burning the fields and raping the womenfolk and stringing him up in the name of democracy, which everybody knew was just another name for slavery that the President in Washington used to make him feel better.

'You stayin' long, sir?'

After *that* – and having been spared, by some miracle or the grace of God – he'd taken to shining shoes for a living, if you could call it a living, when it was really just a surviving and barely that.

The fellow whose shoes he was shining said nothing. He was looking out across the concourse to where a group had gathered, all noisy like soldiers on furlough. Shelby squinted, trying to see, but his eyes could barely see far enough to work; the world beyond the shine was just a blur.

'What?' the man said

Shelby looked up.

The man was staring right at him and frowning. 'I beg your pardon?' he said.

I beg your pardon. Nobody said anything but *nigger* to a black man and certainly not *I beg your pardon*.

'I was just saying wonderin', sir, if yous plannin' on stayin' long...'

Pooley said yes, a couple of months.

'You here for Mardi Gras?'

For a fight, he said.

'A fight? Forgive me for sayin' so, but don't you know you just missed it?'

'What?'

'Well they called it a civil war but there weren't nothin' civil 'bout it, less you call killin' folk to save 'em civil.'

Pooley shook his head, and explained that it was boxing.

'Boxing?'

The Championship of the World.

Shelby Cobb was buffing now, the job not far from done. He paused, looked up. 'This boxing,' he said. 'It's white folks, right? I mean there ain't no niggers involved.'

Pooley shook his head.

Shelby frowned hard. 'So if you's Champion of the World what you *really* is is Champion of the *White* World, there bein' no niggers to beat.'

Pooley smiled.

'Somethin' funny, sir?'

'I was just thinking that maybe you'd like to try it.'

'You mean *boxing*? Ain't you seen how *old* I am?'

'Does it matter?'

'I don't even *know* how old I am – and anyway it matters to *me*. I ain't survived this long just to get my neck broke for the *fi*nancial benefit of white folks.'

'Then come and watch.'

'With you?'

Pooley explained about his cousin and how they had come to the city to train for the fight.

'No, sir,' said Shelby Cobb.

'No?'

'No, sir, I got my ca*reer* and my *future* to consider. I mean, one of these days I intend to meet a lady and have a family of my own and what kind of woman's gonna look at me twice if I give up my empire?'

'That's true,' said Pooley. From across the concourse someone was calling his name. 'Well, if you change your mind—'

'*If?*' said Shelby Cobb. 'What d'you mean *if?*'

'What?'

'You think I'd let you two white boys loose in the city without me to protect you?'

'So you'll come?'

'And this trainin' – where you gonna do that?'

Pooley shrugged. 'Do you know somewhere – somewhere out of the way?'

'You want out of the way?' Shelby Cobb smiled. 'I know a place so out of the way that nobody there knows there ever *was* a way.'

Pooley stood. 'All right then,' he said. 'Meet me here in half an hour.' He turned and walked away.

'Hey…'

He turned.

'Don't think I don't know you didn't pay for that shine.'

Pooley patted his pockets. 'Is later all right?'

Shelby Cobb sighed. Shaking his head, he muttered something sharp and sarcastic, and started packing up his things in preparation for the long journey home.

22

Two days before the fight, Jem and Pooley were out running in the woods when a deer crossed their path, flitting noiselessly from one side to the other and into the low moss-hung trees. The two men stopped and tried to see where it had gone. Then, one way being much like another, they headed after it, taking the route they thought the most likely. After a mile or so they came to the banks of a river. Here they stood breathing hard in the heat and the heavy moist air, quite alone in the simple realm of nature. They looked for the deer but the deer was gone. There were fish swimming free in the river and birds in the low trees overhead. The place was vibrating with life. They lay down on the cool, humming earth.

'So you never did say why you told Hannah to come?' said Pooley after a while. It was a question unanswered from the night before.

Jem said nothing.

'I mean, she comes all this way – *they* come all this way – and now you're here and they're there.'

'So?' said Jem.

'So, what's the point? She's not Adah, and never will be, and she knows it too.'

'It's got nothing to do with Adah.'

'Then *what* does it have to do with? And by the way, what are we going to do if Robert *doesn't* come all this way? Who'll be the corner man?'

'There's plenty. There's you.' Jem pushed himself up. 'You don't have to stay, if you don't like it, you know.'

Pooley pushed himself up also. 'What's the matter with you, Jem? Why do you say these things? Do you want to be alone – in your house with your swanky clothes and three servants? Is that why

Hannah's here? So you know there'll always be somebody around who's too weak to leave? And Ada. She's just a little girl, Jem. She's your *daughter*. Do you even know *how* many children you have?'

Jem was looking out at the water.

'Well?'

'I can't think about any of that,' he said. He looked down at his hands, turned them over then back. 'What if we never go back?' he said.

Pooley turned to look at his cousin's face, just as his cousin caught sight of something. 'Look there,' he said sitting up.

Pooley squinted. There were three, perhaps four ragged figures standing still in the trees on the opposite bank. They were carrying what looked like ancient muskets. At the feet of one was a heap the shape and colour of a deer. One of them called out across the water, his words indecipherable in the thick air.

'What do they want?' said Pooley.

Jem was already standing. 'Did you shoot that thing?' he shouted across.

A voice, muffled: 'Yessir.'

He cupped his hands to his mouth. 'Are you going to eat it?'

Laughter. 'What you reckon, Yankee?'

'Do you have some for us?'

For a moment there was silence. They were turning to each other, clearly deciding.

In the end, one man stepped forward. 'If you got the liquor, Yankee,' he said. 'Then we got the rest.'

And so was the deal concluded.

———◆———

'Do you have everything you want?'

The waiting room is the same one we were shown to when our boy broke his wrist. I remember the Gauguin print on the wall and the crack in the plaster that rises from behind the radiator and gives the whole place a half-derelict feel. It's too warm, which is really the last thing you need, it being the kind of place that makes a person sweat anyway!

'Well, *is* there?' she says.

Like what? I want to say. But instead I say, no, there's nothing.

She pats me on the forearm and before I can say, *Aren't you going to tell me something – anything?* she's gone and it's just me again – me and the little girl.

I turn to the *Notes*.

The little girl's making me nervous, what with her swinging her leg back and forth.

Concentrate. *Concentrate.*

They'd fought in bloody Virginia and had stormed Little Round Top at Gettysburg, where the Union had held on with little more than its will. They had seen their numbers dwindle as the Yankee army grew, and they'd marched barefoot when there'd been no more boots, and seen the glory of war lost in the wilderness and the corpse-strewn mud of Coldharbor. Now they were renegades in their own swamps and bayous, pursued by General Sherman's brutal occupying army.

'So what y'all doin' here?'

The leader of their band was Woody Pearson. Once a Lieutenant in the 12th Louisiana, he'd been wounded in the leg in a fight on a box-bridge in Clinton Missouri and now walked with a limp. He spoke quietly, was a father of six children (four of whom had died from hunger and disease) and was both an educated and a thoughtful man. He knew the war would have been concluded long ago with a share for each side, had the English Queen backed the south, as she'd once promised she would do, and so allowed southern cotton into Lancashire mills and the money coming from it to flow back into Richmond's fast-emptying vaults.

Jem explained about the fight – how he'd come to box an Englishman for the Championship of the World.

'An Englishman?'

And how that Englishman had already lodged his citizenship papers with some government department or other in Albany.

'Albany, *New York*? You mean he's *tryin'* to be a Yankee?'

'My Lord God Almighty,' said a man called Irish Joe, taking a swig from Jem's bottle of sweet Louisiana rye. 'To think there's a man on this earth who's a Yankee that doesn't *have* to be—'

'So when you knock him right down,' said a pale man named

Jonas, who'd not before said a word, 'are you gonna spit in his stinkin' Yankee eye?'

Jem looked to Pooley. 'I don' think spitting's allowed,' he said.

'Not allowed—'

'Calm down now, Jonas,' said the Lieutenant, but Jonas wouldn't calm down.

'You say it ain't allowed to *spit* on a Yankee, when them damned Yankee bastards been rippin' up this country and burnin' it all to hell?' For a moment it seemed like he'd try to hit Jem, but then something inside him broke like a fever and he sat back down and took a swig from the rye.

'I *will* beat him, though,' said Jem. 'You can count on that.'

'You better had,' said Jonas.

'He will,' said Pooley. 'You're looking here at the next Champion of the entire World.'

Lieutenant Pearson raised his bottle. 'I'll drink to that,' he said.

'Me too,' said Irish Joe.

Wouldn't you know, the little girl gets *my news*. Although her mother is whispering, I can tell what she was saying, especially the part about how he didn't suffer and how it was quick and a blessing etc. I feel like saying, 'Hey, that's mine – give it back!' But of course I don't. Instead I just sit here and wait until such time as either my news or my wife arrives, I sit here and turn the page.

I'm suddenly aware of my heart beating, and not entirely in the way one might expect. It flutters like a young girl's on Valentine's night and simply will not settle.

Two beats then nothing. I look hard at the page.

Returning from Magnolia that afternoon, Shelby Cobb found his shack in the woods filled with drunken, sleeping white men.

Amongst them were the two English cousins he'd met at Penn Station, and, in the centre, the remains of a cooked deer. There was snoring and the stink of rye whiskey. He set down his bag and stood a while looking. Then, after watching them for a while, he left the shack and walked away.

He made his way to the dirt road that twisted and turned through the woods on its way to Magnolia, and walked on until he was back amongst the lean-tos and shacks of the town. Here, on promise of future payment, he purchased a gun. Had he been asked why he wanted it, he would have said gladly. But this was America and his right to bare arms was no-one's business but his own.

He held the tall one with the scar in his sights for an hour and, had the man stirred at all, he would probably have fired. It was, after all, the only provocation the man had required when he executed Shelby Cobb's cousin, Abraham. But the man didn't stir, as if he knew, and, when he woke, there was no sign of Shelby Cobb nor any intimation of the death he'd so narrowly avoided.

'How are you feeling?'

'What happened?'

'You had an episode. But at least you were in the right place, eh?'

'An episode?'

'Your heart. It's irregular. The way it beats.'

'Irregular?'

'You need to rest. Sleep. We'll have to shock you tomorrow.'

The click of curtain-rings, the sound of a far-away television. I look around. My clothes are folded on the chair, which means *someone has undressed me*. A monitor beeps above me on the wall, its output irregular, like a man sending maydays from a ship that's going down.

23

THE IRONIES OF life grow abundant and fall beyond a simple man's explanation. Who would have thought, for example, that two Englishmen would be fighting for the championship in America? Or that Shelby Cobb, having returned the gun unused, would abandon the south for New York, where, whilst pursuing his profession at a stand on the concourse at Grand Central Station, he would meet a woman of forty, who was also from Louisiana (not five miles in fact from Magnolia) whom he would marry and with whom, quite unexpectedly, he would have a child? Or that that child's grandchild would one day run unsuccessfully for senator in the state of Illinois, on a platform of tighter gun control and free healthcare for all at the point of need?

'How's your head?'

Jem opened his eyes. His head was pounding. He looked around him. Only Pooley was awake, the others still lying where the food and drink had left them.

'We should run.'

'Run?' He wanted to say *What from?* but then he got Pooley's meaning. He groaned and turned over.

'Come on.'

He shook his head. The toe of a boot struck him hard in the buttocks. *'Hey—'*

'Five minutes.'

'Leave me alone.'

Running was hard, at first, like struggling in heavy boots through mud. But soon his legs were working and his breath was coming close to easy and the bottle's bitter poison was itself on the run. He could feel his muscles working and the strength of his heart and it was glorious. And when they stopped by the river, and the river was running cool, and the early warmth of the sun was like a mother's loving fingers on the back of his neck, he started thinking about things he'd not thought about in years, and how far they'd come and how much further they had to go and how everything turned – their whole lives – on tomorrow.

'Will we do it?' he said.

'Only if we run,' said Pooley, and they did. They ran and ran, and when they got back to the shack, they found the boys awake and already drinking.

'Whatchoodoin'?' said the pale one with the weasel face. Jem looked at Pooley.

'You runnin' like the Yankees you are?' said the mean one, the leader with the scar.

'We're not Yankees,' said Jem.

'Well you sound like Yankees to me. You sure run like Yankees...'

The men laughed. Jem turned again to Pooley. He raised his eyebrow. 'Shall we?' he said.

It was over, the story has it, in the time it takes a thirsty man to drink a whiskey and *when* it was over and the southern boys were nothing but a heap of groaning, ragged flesh, Jem and Pooley took what was theirs from the shack and walked the four miles into Magnolia. Here they sought Shelby with the intention of thanking him for his hospitality. He had been seen hitching a ride on a wagon bound on a route up through Wilcox County. Shelby had said he was heading north, though how far north no-one knew.

'Guess the old fool'll stop when he gets to the ice,' Jackson, the store owner, said, though neither Jem nor Pooley had a clue what he meant.

'So what now?' said Pooley.

Jem shrugged.

'Shall we go and take that belt?'

'What if it doesn't fit?'

'It'll fit around your neck.'

'Hey boys, you want a ride?' Jackson was standing in the store's doorway removing his apron. He'd an errand to run and could head past the station.

When he got there, he stood and watched as the two boys from England climbed onto the train heading south for New Orleans. He raised his arm in a wave as the train pulled away, and felt again that strange aching sadness that he'd felt, even as a young boy, when he'd laid in his bed at night and heard the mournful cry of a distant train.

———◆———

Speaking of ironies – how's this for one? Tomorrow, in order to have my heart stopped and restarted with a regular rhythm, I will be sent to the same ward my father was, when he first arrived all those months ago, and from which he was moved to what will surely be his final resting-place.

On the subject of whom, there is no news.

He's a fighter, people say, in a grotesque mismanagement of the truth. A fighter. Despite the heritage of his great-grandfather, he was never that. If anything he was a giver-upper – except it seems in this case. This is, in itself, a further irony, given that this is the one time I wish he *would* give up and leave me in peace to have my procedure.

I can do nothing but wait. I have a bunch of thrillers that some-body has thoughtfully removed from beside my father's bed and placed beside mine. And, of course, there is always the *Notes*.

I look at my watch to discover it's already four o'clock.

———◆———

The orange-trees were in fruit as the train headed south and on through New Orleans to the town of Kennerville. Here, when they stepped down onto the platform, they could scarcely believe their eyes. The small station was a mass of people – gentlemen with canes and top hats and ladies with parasols, poor folk who'd walked there, the dust still on their boots. There were garlands of flowers – fran-gipani and honeysuckle – draped everywhere and hawkers selling everything from iced tea to cotton scarves. The names of the two fighters were emblazoned on a canvas that stretched for thirty yards from the tree beside the station building to a stake driven hard in the ground.

'Oh my God,' said Pooley.

'Hey, it's them!'

Jem said nothing as a group of fine-suited gentlemen approached. Nor could he speak when those same gentlemen raised him high and pushed their way through the crowd, leaving Pooley to follow as best he could, along with Robert Elke, who'd been waiting there all day for the train to arrive, a note to deliver in his pocket and much to say that had to be said, and soon if it were to mean anything at all.

———•——

'Can you see it?'

I can and here it is. Here *they* are. A century later and here they stand – the two fighters – cast in bronze and bigger than life, only a short bus-ride from New Orleans International Airport.

'Did you say you're related?'

I nodded.

'Bride or groom?'

'What?'

George Sakaris is red-faced and overweight and wearing a *Most Days Are Sunni But Some Days Are Shi'ite* button on his lapel. 'Mace or Allen?'

'Mace,' I say.

'Jeez,' he says. He's wiping his face with a handtowel. 'It sure is hot. Hey, you know the President was here? Stood right here where I'm standing.'

I tell him I didn't.

'Yessir. Right here. Talked about our boys overseas, and how we got to give this war a chance 'cause peace sure as hell didn't work...'

'Do you think he's right?'

'Right?' He smiles. 'Well,' he says, 'he *also* said that we gotta start makin' things here in America, 'cause more and more of our imports are comin' from overseas. What do *you* think?'

'I take it you're not a Republican.'

'You take it right.'

'Are you from around here?'

'I was.'

'*Was?*'

'Until Katrina came by and rearranged things.'

'You lost your house?'

'I lost my house, yessir. Last time I saw it, it was upside down and heading for Mexico. But anyhow you wanna see where it happened – the fight?'

'You know where it was?'

'Isn't hope where wings take dream?'

And so George Sakaris, the now homeless veteran of the US Fourth Infantry's engagement at Dak To, Vietnam, drove us the seven or so miles in the old Buick, in which he now lives, to LaSalle's landing, an old riverboat stop on the banks of the Mississippi. Then, leaving the car, we walked for perhaps a mile upriver to what had once been the old Kenner Farm.

'It was here,' he says.

Before us lies a patchwork of flooded fields – fields that once grew cotton but now seem to grow only waste and despair. The remains of the farm building stand far off to our right, half-walls, a rusted plough in the yard, the hulk of an old car pitched half on its side like a beached submarine. It's a place too hopeless even for ghosts, for even ghosts need some comfort.

The evening creeps in, mist rises from the river. The pale sun that once boiled yellow high over the heads of Jem and Allen, drawing the sweat from their bodies and curses from their mouths, slides low into the water to reveal the great cloth of night.

The clicking of crickets. The noiseless fluttering of bats. Shadows on the land. In the distance a radio, lonesome, inconsolable, like a newly-made widow.

PART THREE

Graves of the Living, Lives of the Dead

24

BUT THERE ARE ghosts whether or not we choose to see them. They are the shadows we leave on the land and on the lives of others; they are burnt into the soil and into the flesh and the bone of those who come after us. We are cumulative, the sum of all that has gone before and something more; we pass through and on, living our lives until a heart fails and the light dims and we are the ghosts, the shadows on the land, the sun-cast tattoos that cannot be erased.

Here's another irony, or perhaps it is just a coincidence.

My son sits before me low on the hard chair, just as I have sat before my father over the last few weeks, And he, like I, can find nothing to say.

There is always a risk: this is how the doctor chose to put it, meaning, I assumed, that if there were things to be said, they should be said and not left for another day.

So.

I ask about his wrist and if it hurts. He shakes his head but won't show me his eyes so I don't know if he's telling me the truth or is just being brave.

'Look,' I say, but my breath lapses. I snake my hand across the covers. His cheek is warm and he does not resist. He lifts his eyes and I know that he's both brave *and* truthful.

'Dad,' he says, 'Mr Fox is back. I left food for him like you do and he came.'

A swish of curtains and the nurse is here and smiling. She looks at my son then at me. 'Is everything all right?' she asks.

'Tell her,' I say. 'Go on.'

He reddens.

CHAPTER TWENTY-FOUR

'Go on.'

'Mr Fox,' he says, 'has come back. He wasn't dead after all.'

I squeeze his hand and, for the first time since his grandmother died, I am reminded how precious and strong our bond is, and it comes back to me how I held him that night as they'd carried her away, and later, much, much later, standing by the window and watching the postman lean his bike against the wall opposite, as if nothing had happened, how death not only comes as a cancer or a speeding SUV, but also through silence and afternoons wasted dreaming in a library, when the world is loud and dancing in the town's sunlit square.

He was taller than Jem and younger and heavier, and had trained until he looked like not a soul in the world could knock him down. He was the Champion and everyone knew it.

As he climbed into the ring, the ring was his and the orange blossom that fell from the trees was his and the people were his, and, as he looked around him, he drew from each upturned face a little more strength, a little more stamina and a little more of the strong scent of victory.

It was as good as over.

'He's already won it,' said Robert Elke, his mouth tight to Jem's ear. 'Look at him he's already parading your belt through the city.'

Jem nodded.

That he's already won it means I've nothing to lose. Jem rose from his stool and raised his fists.

'So can you see them, these ghosts of yours?' George Sakaris cannot see what I can. All he can see is what's real. He cannot see the crowds – the Creole dandies, their glossy coats and leather boots, the woodsmen in their rough shirts, the broad-hatted planters in their suits of white nankeen, the gentlemen from New York and St Louis and Chicago, that latter city's baseball club, who'd come all the way just to be there, quite splendid in their crimson and white, the Louisiana Jockey Club in their mourning clothes of frock coats, twill trousers and top hats. And he cannot see the negroes – hundreds of them – with their calloused hands and feet, and the dark plantation women crowded in the shade of the trees and straining to see the two dumb white men squaring up, and all the hollering and cheering, and the way the old river seemed to care less than nothing for the circus on its banks, and how it kept rolling, just as it rolls today.

'They were my buddies. My brothers. I would have died for them, but I ended up livin'.' As he drives his old Buick back through the battered, beat-up city, George tells me about Dak To, and how he'd lost three-quarters of his squad in a five minute fire-fight on the Cambodian border. He speaks of them with such calmness that the words fall like flowers on a grave, as if to speak of them again – those boys – is to bury them again in the gentlest of graves and to cause them to sleep again like the children they had once been and would never be again.

We arrive at the airport just in time for my flight back to London. We shake hands at the gate. I ask him what he's planning to do – where he'll go, whether he'll somehow try to re-build his home. He shrugs. There's the chance of a place at the VA Centre – it's short term but better than sleeping in a car.

Like a child I look for him as I take my seat but the viewing plat-form on top of the terminal is deserted. I order a drink and listen to the whine of the engines.

Thank you, a voice says, *for visiting the Crescent City*. A sign blinks on, overhead.

I close my eyes. Suddenly, unexpectedly, I long for my family and it comes to me that maybe *that's* what the luck's for – may good fortune shine on me and make everything right after such a long journey – and as we rise and circle above the undefeated city, I look down and think I see, a mile or so from the banks of the grey majestic river, the old Kenner farm and the orange trees in bloom and the high scorching sun, the crowds and the hawkers, and the ring a tiny square, and the fighters rising. For one, it will be the greatest time of his life, for the other it will be nothing but defeat and obscurity, and the knowledge that all that's gone before is worth nothing and that *he's* worth nothing and never will be again...

But that was all ahead for the two of them. The outcome was still to be decided. *Then* there was the noise and the chanting and the first foot forward, and it was Allen – heavy, lumbering, muscle-bound Allen, whose punch could drop a bullock – gracelessly swinging and missing. The crowd went wild as Jem – *the gypsy* – stepped back, and they knew right then he'd be stepping all the way back to England and their money was safe – *just think what I'll make.* Then there he went again, the big man. A left, then a right and this time it connected with a slam you could feel in your guts, and it pushed Jem back until he was up against the ropes – *Get him, you bastard* – and not even five minutes and it was nearly, but not over. There was work to do still, as Jem stepped aside and the big man came on snuffling and panting like a bull, and, for his trouble, took a right to the kidneys that no man should take and a fellow in the third row made a note in his pocket-book and with a nod the odds shortened. Someone called, *Time,* and Robert and Pooley were around him and the water was cold on his throat and *You hurt him,* Pooley said, whether statement of fact or instruction he didn't know, and Robert's hands were on his shoulders and a voice in his ear said, *How much do you want it?* and then he was up and the smell of orange blossom and the sky overhead

was

so

blue

but then there Allen was again, his lips drawn back hard and his sharp yellow teeth, and his arm spinning back and round in a beautiful arc. And Jem stepped aside and into another sudden fist that buckled a rib with a *crack* he could hear, the crowd – *don't they love it* – whooping and hollering as the arcing fist slammed into his cheek, turning him half the way around. He was going down for sure – *just let me sleep* – but something kept him up and when the fist came again, that something ducked him down until he was nearly kneeling and the hurricane overhead had come and gone.

And he stood.

In his head there was silence. He could hear, as clear as day, the fluttering song of a single Green Warbler sitting high in a tree far away across the fields, and see the brown of the tobacco and smell it as if it were right there before him.

But it was not, and all there was was the Champion, who was bleeding from his mouth, but still moving, still coming on. He let another one go and it was wild and the challenger stepped away, but the rope was at his back and suddenly there was nowhere to go…

———————

'Are you ready?'

'Is it time?'

Without consulting his watch the anaesthetist says, 'Bang on.'

Bang on?

'So are you ready?'

'No.'

'Should I take that as a yes?'

'The boy's mother – is she here?'

He nods but a little too gravely. 'Outside,' he says.

'Should I be worried?' I say, but in that moment we're moving, rattling along corridors, through the back and forth of swing doors, and then the hum of the lift.

From behind me and just out of my sight a woman with some kind of accent says, 'Maybe yes, maybe no.' Who she's talking to I don't know.

The lift pings and the doors open and we're travelling again, rattling like a car in some ancient house of horrors, and into the theatre where it's all soothing greens. A woman – maybe the one from the lift – is leaning over me with cool mountain mint breath and smiling, and there's hissing and a mask and a jab – *just a little prick, alright?* – and it's ten, nine, eight, seven, si

25

IN EVERY LIFE, a moment of axis – a year, a minute, a second – that changes and defines all that follows: a bus just missed, a letter unposted or lost in the mail, a wedding bouquet unexpectedly caught in bright summer sunlight. It's a chance meeting in the gloom of a library, or a moment's hesitation a hundred years ago in a ring on the banks of the Mississippi River – a second's eye-to-eye, as two men, who are killing each other and themselves for the benefit of their audience, realize their foolishness and, for a single, fleeting moment, know the truth: that they're brothers and should sit down together and find a way out...

'Hey, Jem, you've *got* him—'

...but then that moment *in* that moment is gone, and it's too late, and it was Jem, who, though older, was also less sated with soft beds and fine food, that woke first from the fantasy, and raised his aching fists and, like a child, struck wildly at all he could see – and all he could see through half-closed eyes was a frail and frightened man in front of him who was bloody and stooped. *It's me or it's him*, he told himself, *it's me or it's him, and it's not going to be me*. With a blow to the man's side and another to his head that sent a cascade of sweat and blood and mucus over both of them like confetti – *we are gathered here today* – and the sounds of choking and gargling consistent with a glorious punch to the throat, and the wonderful ruin of a voice that had once, when very, very young, whispered *I love you* to a mother in mourning for a man, who'd never once taken her hand except in anger or offered her his – a voice that would whisper no more to anyone, and especially to a mother who'd been dead these long years. And with that blow and more, another and another and another sent the two men reeling back into the cage, from which for a moment they'd been sprung and swung the door behind them and locked it for good and it was over.

'Hello? Can you hear me?'

A face – dark, Indian, Pakistani, Iraqi, Kuwaiti, who knows? – is hanging like a lantern before me. White teeth. Beautiful teeth. Why do dark-skinned people always have beautiful teeth?

A hand squeezes mine. I move my eyes left like the turret of a tank. A woman I don't know, or at least don't remember. She's crying or has been and though confused, I'm certain this is not what's expected and I'd like to say, '*Do you mind?*' But I can't speak thanks to the tubes and, even if I could, what's the point? She's here and she's plainly not planning to leave. Great. I close my eyes. *Take the hint, why don't you.* She doesn't. She squeezes my hand again and says something I don't catch and don't try to, but then everything's so hazy suddenly. I close my eyes again and there's blackness, a kind of buzzing, then whistling like wind through an underground car park, then nothing but the whooping and yelling and the silence at the core of it that was Jem, and how through the blood and bruises and broken ribs he was trying to hear *really* hear what Pooley was saying and what Robert Elke was saying and what *everyone* was saying – that he, James Mace, from Beeston in Norfolk, who'd sat in the loft in the Old Cutter Barn and dreamed one day he'd be Champion *was* Champion now today this very moment, and not just Champion but *Champion of the Whole Wide World*. And it wasn't until they raised him up and he was riding high on their shoulders and he could feel the still-warm sun on his face and taste the salt of his own blood that he *could* really hear it and really believe it and, though he knew instinctively, and with that beautiful sadness, that this was near the end of things, and not the beginning, and that he was three-quarters done.

He knew also that you're a fool if you think too much and waste too much time worrying, and that you only get one time around and you'd better make it count...

'It's your father.'

'What about him?'

Nurse Bellingham shakes her head.

CHAPTER TWENTY-FIVE

'He's dead?'

How strange it is that so much can be said by not saying a single thing.

'I'm so sorry.'

'It was while I was—'

This time a nod. 'He slipped away. There was no pain. One minute he was there—'

'Where is he now?'

'No, I meant—'

'No, *I* meant is he still on the ward—'

She says she doesn't know, that she'll find out. She turns to go but glances at the woman by the bed, then at me, and pauses.

'Will you be all right?' she says.

He slipped away. There was no pain.

I look hard at the woman. 'Will I?' I say, Heaven knows why.

'I hope so,' she says sweetly.

'Look, who are you?' I say. It just comes out.

She glances at the nurse, as if asking permission for something.

There was no pain.

'I was your father's friend.'

He slipped away.

'Friend?'

Another glance.

'Not his *wife* then,' I say. 'Someone told me that's what you've been saying.'

She looks suddenly crestfallen, as if I've taken something from her that she'd wanted to give.

'Well?'

He's dead.

'Yes.'

'Yes?'

'I'm sorry.'

'For what?'

'I should have waited.'

'*Waited for what?*'

'The right time.'

Now I'm losing what's left of my strength. The nurse steps towards me.

'If she doesn't tell me what she's talking about and right now...' I peter out, short of breath, knowing what is coming but not wanting to.

'Your father and I are – *were* – married.'

'Right. And now he's dead.'

'What?'

I knew it. Dead. Married. 'Anything fucking else?'

She looks shocked, and I can feel my newly re-started heart flipping out, but then it settles – it's thumping like a crazy thing but regularly, at least.

'You should rest,' says Nurse Bellingham. 'You've had a shock.' For a second I think she's joking, but she's not. The poor woman probably wishes she'd stayed in bed – both of them do, no doubt.

I know I should apologize but I don't, I can't. The truth is I'm not sorry – about anything. *I'm not sorry because I don't care.* That burden has somehow been lifted from me. 'You can all go to hell,' I say, or something like it. I can't remember exactly what. All I *do* remember is having to take a piss and being too late and feeling the warmth creeping over my thighs, and it crossing my mind for no reason whatsoever that I can think of, how great it would be to take a weekend in Shanghai, or a month with my mate on the Gold Coast, wearing nothing but boardies and a new pair of Nikes.

'The where?' a voice says. 'What's he saying?'

Then muffled sounds and the feeling that everything's moving, then another voice, 'Oh, Jesus, he's pissed himself', and then it's Tuesday and I'm sitting on the terrace in the sunshine, and I'm waiting for mother and son to return, though where they've been I can't for the life of me remember.

The journey back to the City, my father wrote in the *Notes*, was delayed by a visit to Natchez, the oldest settlement on the Mississippi River – the oldest and most notorious, due to the fact that there were more ways to gamble your money there, and lose it, than pretty much anywhere else known to man. Which is what Jem did, because he was a fool, and because now he'd had some and he was certain there'd be more. He knew this for no reason other than it had been his observation that money always goes to money, and that if you don't have it, but somehow still manage to acquire it, then you're in, and for good, and you just have to settle back and count it, as it rolls right through your door.

Which, for a while at least, it did. The public want to see for themselves the person that's making the news, until the next person comes along.

And so they did. They paid to see the Champion from one coast to another, and from the Mexican border and up into Canada. But their admiration was neither genuine nor free. They paid to watch him striking poses on a stage, and he paid for the whiskeys in the bar. Women queued to be seen with him – this brutal dandy of a man – and had sex with him to make something of themselves, or through boredom or fear of some onrushing, sensationless oblivion. There were other fights too, of course – the ill-matched contests familiar today. For the moment, Mace was an industry, and his status as Champion was good business. And, by the time he arrived with Pooley in the city of Boston, this 'Champion of America' was the indirect source of much cash for some of the most unpleasant men in America.

Which is not to say that he didn't have fun, just that fun – sex, new shirts, swanky hotel rooms – had somehow become the point of it all. Gone were any thoughts of where he'd come from, or any concern for his wives and children. His ignorance had been found out and he celebrated it. He didn't know where Boston was – couldn't have found it on a map – but who cared? What did it matter that the America that had loved him when he'd come to be beaten, hated him now that he'd won? Certainly they paid well to see him, but mostly they paid to put flesh to the fiend. They wanted their own, an *American* Champion – not a man from a country whose grandees had so recently had them in chains, nor a counterfeit American like Allen. America was grown up, and had come through the fire, and needed their own man. That man's name was Coburn.

Joe Coburn was a big man in Boston, and Boston was big in the fight game. It was also the most dangerous city in America – a city of crime awash with guns, a place with an underworld so pitiless and a police force so corrupt that, should a man find himself under threat in his home, from an intruder with a pistol and the willingness to use it, there was nothing he could do but look for justice in the next world. To look for it in this one was to look in vain. So bad was the city's security and so likely was an attempt on Jem's life, that an alternative venue had to be found.

Much as Las Vegas owed its growth during the forties and fifties to the need of the New York mafia for a new and distant territory to exploit, Kansas City owed much to the crime syndicates of the city of Boston, a century or so earlier. It was a place of few rules and little law – an ideal location, therefore, for organized crime's country home.

An ideal location, too, for the fight of the century.

Mace vs. Coburn.

England vs. America.

Vanquished master vs. Uppity slave.

Articles were signed and arrangements made. Nobody knew, of course, who would win, except those who would always win. The fight would be the engine behind the shift of great fortunes westward. Vast bets were made and lives mortgaged to fund them.

'Are you the Englishman?'

And all on the hearts and bodies of two men.

Jem said, yes, he supposed he was. 'But my friends are also,' he said. 'Perhaps you're looking for one of them.'

Bracing himself against the movement of the train, the young man glanced from one face to the next. 'No, sir,' he said, returning to the first, 'I believe it's you I'm looking for. You *are* Mr Jem Mace the Boxing Champion, aren't you?'

'He is,' said Pooley. 'Champion of the World. And who are you?'

The young man straightened and put out his hand. He was tall and lean and had a seriousness about him that made you think he'd either end up being somebody, or die trying. 'My name's Earp,' he said.

Jem rose. They shook.

'But you can call me Wyatt. If you like that is.'

'It's a pleasure Mr Earp,' said Jem, aware of sniggering behind him. 'Are you with us for the fight?'

The young man shook his head. 'No, sir. At least I *may* be. I have a job on the railroad just outside the city. I'm hoping I can make it. It sure would be a fine sight to see.'

'I suppose,' said Jem, 'you'll be backing my opponent. Perhaps you've even placed a bet—'

'A fool if he has,' said Pooley.

'A bet? No, sir.' The young man looked grave. 'I never wager, sir, as I can never be sure of the outcome.'

Jem smiled.

'Although people do say the lucky dollar's on you.'

'Is that right?'

'Yes, sir.'

Jem sat down. He pointed to a spare seat across the way beside the window. 'Would you join us?'

The young man's face lit up, exposing the youth behind the serious façade. 'You mean it?'

'You can tell us all about where we're going. I hear it's quite a town.'

Wyatt Earp made his way past the sleeping Robert Elke and took his place by the window. The land was flat and brown and dry, the mountains in the distance silver blue. It was the start of the West, the place of man's return to his distant, primitive past.

26

HAD IT NOT been for the ten-second bloodbath in a sordid backyard called the OK Corral, when a few stupid men got killed and others did the killing, Wyatt Earp might well have gained his fame simply by having somehow survived as a lawman in the most violent and lawless place in the American West, at the most violent and deadly time in its grim and terrible history.

But that was all ahead. On that train heading out to Kansas City, he was a young man with neither fear of the future, nor yet knowledge of the power of the past.

———•———

'So where's your mum?'

My son says he doesn't know, but I doubt that. I think it more likely that she's bribed him into silence and will simply come home when she chooses to. Which is not to say that she's a monster, and entirely uncaring of the fact that my father has recently died, but simply just more evidence of the breakdown of our life together.

On the other hand, perhaps she's actually stopped off to buy Chinese food and a bottle of Semillon Chardonnay, and is planning to surprise me with tickets for a week in the Seychelles.

I get a call from my father's best man, Sasha (the first time round, that is), to tell me that he's uncovered a photograph of my father as a young boy in the arms of Jem Mace, and is sending it in the mail, so it should be here tomorrow. Which is something to look forward to.

———•———

'That's the Missouri River,' said the young man. 'And that – *this* – is the Hannibal and St Joseph Railroad Bridge. Been open five years and already had three people jump right off it.'

From the window, Jem looked down at the brown Missouri River. It was hard to see anything through the driving rain. They could have been anywhere.

He sat back. 'How do you know all these things?' he said. The young man had barely paused in his talking in the two hours since he'd joined them. 'I thought you were from the East.'

'I am, sir. But I like to learn. I like to know where I'm going.'

'You don't like surprises?'

'No, sir. Do you? When you take to the ring, don't you like to know who you're fighting? I mean, if he's tall or short, or fast or slow? Take this Coburn fellow. I'll bet you know things about *him* even his mama don't know.'

Jem shrugged. He felt like sleeping. For two hours he'd felt like sleeping. 'Well I know he's Irish,' he said.

'Is he tall?'

'I believe so.'

'Are your arms a match for his? I mean are they longer or shorter?'

Jem hadn't a clue and he said so. 'I *also* don't know,' he said, 'if he likes his meat roasted or turned in a pan. Or if he wears a top hat or smokes a cigar. Do you think I should?'

The young man reddened. He had clearly stepped over some unseen line. He was about to apologize, when the brakes beneath them squealed and the train pulled into the station.

Jem leaned forward. 'Forgive me,' he said, and he patted the young man's knee. 'I get a little tensed up sometimes. I'm sure you understand.'

Wyatt Earp nodded. He'd know tension of his own one day – but not yet. Now, for him, everything new was simply something to be explored. He cupped his hands to the window. 'This is the West,' he said, his breath clouding the glass.

The train emptied slowly. Pooley and Robert Elke had to drag themselves from sleep. They stood on the platform a little fuzzy-headed, none of them knowing quite what to do.

'Yes?' asked Jem. Wyatt Earp was standing a little way off, something clearly on his mind.

'Well,' he said, 'if you're looking for some place to stay the night, I believe there's a hotel at 12th Street and Campbell Avenue.'

'There is?'

'I believe so.'

Jem turned to Pooley, who shrugged.

'If you like, I could show you...'

He turned back. 'I don't suppose you know,' he said, 'what with you being as much of a stranger here, as I am, where I might find some gunpowder and whiskey?'

Wyatt Earp let a smile creep over his face. 'Gunpowder and whiskey?' he said. 'Excuse me, but I do believe you've come to the very best place in the world for them goods, and I'd be honoured to help you attain them.'

'Lead on, then,' said Jem, and so the young man did, out of the low wooden station and on into the mud of the town – much as one day, in years to come, he would walk through those same ragged streets, in the company not of Englishmen, but his brothers Virgil and Morgan, and a lean, consumptive dentist named Doc Holiday.

———————

I have leaned the picture against the wall on the mantle more in hope than expectation that it will speak to me in some way. Thus far, it has not. Thus far, it is as dumb as Whistler's Mother, and considerably less colourful.

But it's early days.

People keep saying this with reference to recent events, as if they're telling me something I don't already know. *You'll get over it,* they say. *Give it time.* Which, in my case, is bullshit. I'm *already* over it and will *never* get over it, regardless of how many weeks or months or years have passed. After all, do you say to a man who's halfway through a life sentence, *Don't worry you'll get over it?*

I think not.

What I *do* think is that, should the boy's mother return, then a number of things will need to be established. Rules if you like. For example, there must be no more filling the his head with nonsense about how his grandfather was so brave to bear what he did, when he had no choice but to do so.

Also, when this ridiculous business has run its course, and the ashes are available, there must be *absolutely no way* that they will be mixed with those of his first wife, my mother. What happens to them is otherwise of no consequence to me.

And one other thing.

Should anyone else care to mention how generous it was of him to give me the *Notes* before he pissed and dribbled his way out of existence, then may they be the last. Just because I have yet to figure out why it was a bad thing to do, doesn't mean it wasn't. The only good thing he ever did for me was buy me a brand-new pair of binoculars when I was ten. After that? Nothing. So don't think I'm fooled.

Speaking of the *Notes*, I have done some research and discovered that Kansas City is not only the most centrally placed city in the entire continental United States but also the wettest. And that the day that was scheduled for the Mace-Coburn fight was the wettest of the whole year. This goes some way to explaining why the fight was, at once, so brutal and so much a farce.

Picture this. A ring on the outskirts of the city – with a rope but no canvas flooring, meaning that, by the time they were scheduled to begin, the ground was a quagmire, and so swollen with rainwater that, in some places, a man could sink down to his ankles and above. And then there was the rain itself. If you arrived at the fight in the company of a blonde, the architect George Kessler later said, then the chances were, visibility being so poor, that you'd end up going home with a redhead. All of which must have given Jem some cause for concern, it being *his* crown and *his* belt on the line. But what could he do? To pull out would be to forfeit, and he'd not come this far to end it all with another charge of cowardice. He would fight come Hell or high water and, though the latter was already very much in evidence, he could never have guessed that the former was also on its way.

The fight began in the usual fashion, except insofar as the usual circling and sizing up had all the gravitas of a pantomime. Both fighters slipped and nearly fell, and it wasn't until perhaps twenty minutes of inaction had passed and the huge, sodden crowd had grown so restless that some in the audience threatened to reach for their pistols (and *some* actually *did*), that Jem struck the first blow and sent the Irishman stepping back in surprise.

And only then did the real fight begin.

Coburn jabbed and Jem swung his fist, connecting first with the Irishman's left eye and then his nose, closing the first and splitting the second, and the man's face that was running with rain was suddenly running red too. But he jabbed and jabbed harder and low, too, hitting Jem in the groin. Jem half buckled, but didn't call foul. Instead he forced himself up and threw another at Coburn's bloody face, and this time his lip split wide and the pulse of blood increased, until his chest was running thick with it, but it drove him on and he pushed the Champion back with a hard combination that rocked him and pitched him back against the rope. Then Coburn was upon him and had Jem down, and he would have stayed down had the boot to his groin not made him so mad that his anger was stronger than his pain. Jem rose and started swinging, and wouldn't even stop when a voice that seemed so distant, but was just a yard away, called out *Time!* and Robert Elke's arms were around him and dragging him back, and he was sitting in his corner, and the rain was teeming down, and everything he'd ever known was gone, and there was just that moment, just the rain and the salt of his blood. How he longed to close his eyes, and he did, and there he was, suddenly walking the lanes again, with Pooley at his side, and dragging a chair across a cold, stone floor, then climbing up and lifting the latch *so quietly that no-one would hear—*

'*Hey, Jem, are you listening?*'

But then the past was all gone and he was standing again, and the rain was still falling, and he took a step forward, slam into a fist that spun him hard and right around, showering the front rows with blood and sweat, and he knew in that moment, in the way you can *know* something by *feeling* it, that if anything was going to do it, if anything was going to finish him then this was it and he waited and waited. And, when he didn't go down, he knew the day was his, he just had to make the man know it. How could he do this, except hit as hard as he knew how, hit even with his left hand, that was swollen and bloated with pus, smearing the man yellow and fouling the air? And even when arms wrapped around him and drew him to his corner, and a voice in his ear said *It's over*, it wasn't nearly over, but when he tried to get up, his legs were gone and he couldn't have stood, not even to save himself, and he tried to speak but he couldn't speak, and only when Pooley was right there before him did he *know* that it was over and he'd never get to do this again in his life, never get to hurt this bad. It made him want to cry and he *did* cry but the rain hid his tears and he drew Pooley in close and half-spat, half-whispered something in Pooley's ear that made him draw back and shake his head. Jem squinted through the rain to where Coburn was sitting. Coburn was a mess, his chest as bloody as a butcher's apron, his face red and pulsing as if the flesh of it had been stripped of its skin. He drew his focus back to Pooley.

The referee had called it a draw.

He opened his mouth; Pooley nodded as if hearing the unspoken question. 'Yes, it's time to go home,' he said.

'Home?' said Jem, the word just a rattle in his throat. *But home isn't there any more,* he wanted to say, *and anyway even if it was...*

But then arms were moving him, and carrying him in the rain, and everything was dancing around him and how long he didn't know. He could feel the rhythm of a train's wheels beneath him, and whether or not he was sleeping, and whether or not his mother's kiss, planted cool on his forehead was real or not, he couldn't have said, but he knew it didn't matter, because a kiss is a kiss, and just as a mother is born with the birth of a child, so she dies only when he dies, and he wasn't dead yet, and it was the pain that made him know that for sure...

'Jem?'

When he woke and it was day and the rain was gone and the skies were clear, he knew something had changed in him. When he looked at the faces around him, he wondered who'd died, and he pushed himself up and said, 'Pooley?'

Pooley was frowning. Beside him, quite round in his uniform, with a red face and whiskers, stood a police officer with a pistol on his hip. 'How are you feeling, sir?' he asked.

Jem glanced at Pooley. 'I'm all right,' he said. 'I think. Aren't I?'

'He'll be fine, officer,' said Pooley.

The officer nodded. 'So did you recognize them?' he said.

'Who?'

'The men at the station,' said Pooley. 'Don't you remember?'

'No. What men?'

'You don't remember the guns – the noise?'

He shook his head.

'They were from New York,' said the officer with obvious disdain. 'And as good a shot as you might expect.'

Jem looked hard at his cousin. 'What the hell is he talking about?'

'There were three of them,' said Pooley. 'They came out of nowhere. Missed you by the width of my hand and smashed a light. There was glass everywhere – even in my hair. Look…' He leaned forward, parting his thinning hair and displaying the cuts on the high part of his temple.

Jem shook his head. 'I don't remember a thing,' he said, and truly he didn't. All he could remember as he lay there in his room at the hotel on 12th Street and Campbell Avenue wasn't really a memory at all, but something told to him as a child that had since *become* a memory.

'Jem?'

And in that moment, in that memory, his father was before him again, leaning back against his bench in the smithy, his dark arms ribbed with veins, his face flushed with the heat of the furnace.

'Young Wyatt's here to see you. He'd like to speak to you.'

Remember, he was saying, how Richard Nockolds, the scoundrel, who'd been a sword and a shield to the working man, had turned a dozen times on the rope that had hanged him, but with every turn had tightened the noose around the necks of the wealthy, and remember too how every life ends just the same, and what matters is what a man's done, not the cruel and bitter nature of his end.

Jem opened his eyes. 'Mr Earp,' he said. 'Forgive me for not rising.'

Wyatt Earp stepped forward, his hat in one hand, a small pine box in the other. 'I heard what happened,' he said.

'At the fight?'

'At the station, sir. I heard how those boys tried to kill you.'

'Well they missed.'

'Do you know who they were?'

Jem glanced at Pooley then back. 'Maybe the train being late made them mad. Do you think, Pooley?'

'Maybe. Anyway I believe our friend here has something for you.' He nudged the young man.

'Yes I do, sir.' He stepped forward another pace and opened

the box. Inside, fitted snugly in faded red velvet, lay a pistol with a polished wooden handle and a barrel of dark metal. 'It was one of my daddy's,' he said. 'And I know he'd have wanted you to have it.'

With the help of his cousin, Jem pushed himself up. 'I can't take it,' he said.

'Well I can't take it back.'

'What if I shoot somebody?'

The young man shrugged. 'My daddy says if you shoot somebody, you make sure you shoot them dead.'

Jem took the box and laid it on his lap. He thanked the young man and watched him leave. Later that night, as the western moon rose and lit the room through the open window with its pale silver light, he thought again about his father, and it occurred to him that the closer his father had got to the end, the more like a boy he'd seemed to become – the more afraid, the more frightened by the world. As he closed his eyes and waited for sleep, he could feel in the slow, gentle breath of the breeze, the whisper of his own death, and he realized then how a man is a fool, who abandons his family, and relies for his strength on the shallow care of strangers.

27

WHETHER OR NOT it was fear of a lonely death that made him pack up and return at once to New York, without any thought to a re-match with Coburn, Jem's reunion with Hannah and Ada, when he *did* return to the city, it was both brief and unsatisfactory. He had only been back a month when something of the old Jem returned. Reports began to filter back to Hannah that her husband had been seen in the company of this or that woman, or that a certain club on the West Side, or in Brooklyn, had been honoured by a visit from the reigning World Champion, when he should have been elsewhere and home before dawn. That these reports came mostly from those with reason to despise the cocky Englishman mattered little. To Hannah they were all too credible and only served to confirm what she'd already come to fear. Jem couldn't be trusted and that was the end of it.

Neither, it seems, could his life be guaranteed. Friends of Joe Coburn made it known that an assassin, or assassins, had been paid in advance to shoot the World Champion dead, and throw his weighted-down body into the East River. It was, they made it known, for the honour of the Irish, whose alleged mistreatment by the English over centuries was perfectly illustrated by the underhand tactics of the gypsy from Norfolk. What these lamentable tactics were they never said. As usual, a primitive call to arms was enough to inflame Irish hearts, and consequently Jem was no longer safe on the streets of New York.

It was time to get out.

'And this was it?'
'The very one.'

Now ironically an Irish-themed pub, Jem's Bare-knuckle Bar and Grill still retains many of its original features. Still there is the great oak bar, which came all the way from Tennessee, against which the fighter would pose and greet important customers as they entered the place. This he did for the young Teddy Roosevelt, who, on returning from a family holiday to Europe, sought him out and raised to him a fulsome and generous toast in honour of the great country of his birth, and from whom he took instruction in the basics of boxing, so that there should be no repeat of the bullying he'd suffered as a boy. It was also here against the bar that former President, Ulysses S. Grant, was leaning, when a captain retired from the 20ᵗʰ Maine, approached him. The man had fought so heroically at the Battle of Gettysburg, but now begged to be relieved of his command fully, nearly twenty years after the battlefield had fallen silent.

'So why did he leave?'

We're sitting at the bar – David Leiber and I – watching ice hockey on TV.

'Because a man with a gun was after him. Which is a good reason. And because he was a terrible husband and father. Which is another good reason.'

'Except for the wife and child.'

'*Especially* for the wife and child.'

On the TV the Toronto Maple Leafs go two up against the Flames.

'Did he take the gun?'

'Wouldn't you?'

'Did he ever fire it?'

'Who knows?'

Three up.

'So where did he go?'

'San Francisco. He and Pooley were planning to go to Oz and New Zealand. Got as far as Virginia City.'

'Where's that?'

'Nevada.'

'What's there?'

'You don't know?'

David shrugs. So what *is* there?'

'No idea.'

'There must have been something.'

And there was. As of the summer of 1859 there was silver and lots of it, courtesy of the Comstock Lode Strike. And with silver came money, and with money came gambling, and with gambling boxing, and for Jem the offer of a purse of one thousand pounds if he would take on the local man Bill Davis.

'What about the wife?'

Hannah was pregnant and too sick to make the journey west, so she stayed in New York with Ada and wasn't there to see Jem, Pooley and Robert off at the station. They didn't know when they'd be returning. For Hannah it was another abandonment. For Jem it was another escape.

'Wasn't it dangerous?'

Only ten years before, the journey coast to coast had been long and fraught with danger – indeed, so frequent were the instances of kidnap and murder by 'renegade' Indians, that the numbers travelling began to decline.

'Custer?'

However, the slaughter of General Custer at the Little Big Horn turned things around. The American people began clamouring for revenge – revenge for which a supine Congress gladly stumped up the dollars. Regiments were raised in support of a policy better known today as ethnic cleansing. This, combined with the cynical introduction of vast quantities of cheap whiskey to the squalid and inhuman reservations, neutralized the threat of attack, until the threat was no more vivid than that posed by drunks in a public park at noon.

'And so they went.'

And so they went, the two cousins and Robert Elke, Jem and Pooley spending hours at a time on the roof of the train, while Robert slept below in the carriage. They marvelled at the vast green pastures of Kentucky and the thoroughbred horses with their slim muscled torsos. And when the train slowed and climbed through the Rockies, the air was so clean it was like they were the first ever to breathe it. The cold burned their faces and they laughed like the children they'd once been long ago in the lanes around Beeston. Riding so high was like riding on top of the world, and when they began to descend, and Virginia City came into view, they felt made anew – as if the grime of New York and all that was or had ever been bad in their lives had been washed away. For a moment they were children again, and all was as simple as it once had been.

———

'So what now?'

'In what sense *what now?*'

'Well, do you go home?'

'*Or?*'

'*Or* do you not.'

It's a good question and one that's been nagging at me since the call this morning. Asking David what he'd do would be pointless. What he'd do is obvious. *He'd do the right thing.* Which, in his case, would be home and the much-delayed funeral, and to hell with Virginia City.

Which is, of course, what I'll do.

'I've decided,' I say.

'And?' he says.

'Do you think a dark tie with a dark suit is *de rigueur* – or can I lighten it up with some colour?'

28

NEARLY SIX THOUSAND people watched the bout in Virginia City. Almost all of them were miners and most of them were armed and excited by the combination of drink and just about the only distraction from scrabbling in the dirt to have come their way since the arrival of the railway. And so, when after just on half an hour, their man Bill Davis was beaten fair and square, and retired from the ring in honourable defeat, most of those guns were raised up to the sky and fired several times, until the air was thick with gunsmoke and the hard, dusty ground was quite awash with empty shells.

Particularly for Jem, but for Pooley and Robert Elke too, Virginia City meant the start of a whole different life. Gone were the fights fought in driving rain or the terrible sapping heat of the bayou, or those against men who fought as if their lives and the lives of their families depended on victory – in their place came opponents for whom it was enough just to spar with the great man and to smile in defeat. This was boxing as entertainment and not barely-disguised attempted murder. And there were plenty of takers for this, and a reasonable living to be made. For Jem, this included a rematch with Bill Davis further west in California, just a month after the first.

This fight, like the first, ended in victory for the Champion, and with every soul in attendance paying a dollar for entry, and between five and fifty dollars for a seat, the night lined Jem's pockets with more money than he'd ever known, without him having suffered a single solid blow.

When he left the city hundreds gathered at the wharfside, as the SS *Sonoma*, bound for Melbourne blew its steamhorns and prepared for the long Pacific voyage.

CHAPTER TWENTY-EIGHT

'How do you know when you're in San Francisco?'

I try, but not hard, to raise a smile.

'Well?'

'I don't know,' I say. I'm scanning the screen for my flight.

The fat man with the bushwhackers hat leans in close and drops his voice. 'You know it,' he whispers, 'when your hairdresser's straight, your plumber's a pooftah, the woman who delivers your *mail* is straight, and your Avon lady's a guy in drag – that's how you know it, buddy!'

Last call.

'I have to go,' I say.

'Go?'

'My flight.'

'Melbourne?'

My heart sinks. 'You too?' I say.

'Me too,' he says, and the day is complete.

It began with a phonecall home and the news that – not unexpectedly – due exclusively to my absence – the funeral was a farce. No-one spoke except the vicar, who gave my father the wrong name, and was under the impression that he'd fought with the Desert Rats in Libya in 1942, when in fact he'd been watching the clouds in the Meteorological Office in Whitehall, and the only action he'd seen had been the coming together of nimbus and cumulus in the skies above Saipan. Of course there was also the extra burden placed on my sister, which I do regret, but it couldn't be helped.

'You been before?'

I lift my earphones.

'Melbourne! You been before?'

'*Neighbours*,' I say. 'That count?'

I replace my earphones. Michael Buble. *You are not alone...*

I close my eyes. I feel like crying. *It's over*, I tell myself. *Thank God it's all over.* In a while I sit up. The fat man's asleep. I open the *Notes. On arrival in Australia*, I read but something stops me.

All over.

From nowhere it has suddenly come to me that it's *not* all over at all, and it comes to me also high up above the ocean on the other side of the world that it'll *never* be over and it will always be with me – that moment of abandonment in my father's flat, as vivid as a scar, and as quietly and inexorably corrupting as a cancer's tiny hands.

However, there's nothing to do but carry on. Keep looking. Keep searching. Keep reading the *Notes*, written as they are in his spidery hand.

So.

＊

On arrival, he says, in Australia, there were ten thousand people on the quayside, nine thousand or so there to gawp at and cheer for a man they'd never seen before, but whose face they knew from a hundred artist's drawings. If ever there were an indication of how far away from the world they felt themselves to be, this was it. They were hungry for something, *anything*, from home, and would follow it anywhere and cheer it until they were hoarse.

For Jem, such a greeting was a revelation and the pickings, he knew, were certain to be rich. Aside from the exhibitions he was scheduled to give, people flocked in their hundreds to hear him speak about his life – and not only that. They came too to hear the Champion play his fiddle, and to marvel at how a man with such stained and battered hands could wield a bow with such a lightness of touch, how he could produce in his listeners feelings so mournful that they'd cry for a homeland they'd never seen, and painfully revive loves long forgotten.

In his first month in Australia, Jem boxed close to thirty exhibitions and gave so many talks that his voice took a pounding his body had never done. He fought an exhibition match underground in a silver mine and, for his trouble, was presented by the miners with a block of solid silver inscribed with the words *Here is a Brick and You are Another*. When not exhibiting his 'new style' of boxing, he'd talk about his early life and introduce his cousin Pooley, and together they'd describe Beeston and the church and the flat Norfolk country, and their desire when still boys to escape their narrow lives and make something grand for themselves. This always raised a cheer wherever they went, as did Jem's vivid story of Pooley's terrible sickness, caused by the pitching of a boat on The Wash. Jem spoke also of his mother and his brothers and how much he missed them. He never spoke, though, of his father, or of his wives. Talk of the latter would, perhaps, have lowered his rate of success with the ladies, many of whom would earn a modest but usual sum from their tales of their nights in his arms. Why he never spoke of his father, on the other hand, is impossible to say for sure. Perhaps he felt guilty about his absence at the time of the old man's death. Or perhaps not. Maybe it was something else that he never shared.

—•—

'So where now?'

'What do you mean?'

'Do you have a place to stay?'

Yes, I say, an old college friend. The fat man seems disappointed.

I say *Goodbye*, shake his hand and head for the cab rank. Without needing to look back, I know for certain he is watching me. He's clearly lonely and that made me want to scoot.

I slam the car door, bark an address and in a second he is gone – just a fat man in a silly hat.

29

THE WILD WEST without guns is what one traveller called the Outback, and so it was in a sense. There were dust-covered one street towns and undernourished horses tied to rails outside saloons, and the kinds of characters that only ignorance and isolation or maybe John Ford could create. There were fistfights and jealousies, and land left unexplored by all but the strange-looking natives that seemed to stretch out to the edge of the world and over.

It was the kind of land that, as he had got older, had come to appeal to Jem more and more. There was a flatness to it that took him back to Norfolk and his days as a boy, and an *out there* feeling that both thrilled and repelled him. With Robert not feeling so well (he had pains in his side that were coming more and more frequently), and Pooley needing to organize his engagements, Jem would often leave them behind in the city and hitch a ride on a wagon-train heading north, packing only some food and his fiddle. Wherever he stopped, what people there were would gather around him, not because they knew of him (for very little from the outside world reached them), but just to hear him play, payment for which would take the form often of a tender smokehouse rabbit or a blanket on the floor for the night. Jem would tell them of the sights he'd seen – of New York and its skyscrapers and the London of Dickens and the Queen – and when the time came to leave, he'd shake hands with everyone, jump up beside the driver of a city-bound wagon and take the comfort of a gypsy – the knowledge that he'd never be back.

It was during one of these rides – this time back to Sydney and a two-month 'entertainment' engagement at the Queen's Theatre – that Jem first heard the name Abe Hicken.

Hicken was an Englishman by birth and was that rare combination of coward and prize-fighter. After an early career in his native Birmingham, he had moved to America, drawn by the money then awash in the prize-fighting world: not unreasonably he fought only those opponents whom his spies had convinced him would be easily beaten. He had then fled all the way to Australia, before the husband of a lady from Cleveland could catch up with him and make good on a threat of revenge involving dogs trained for fighting and a short length of rope.

Once in Sydney, he proclaimed himself 'Champion of Australia' (this with considerable *chutzpah*, considering he fought only two fights for real and fabricated a dozen more) and then promptly retired, adopting the position of elder statesman of the fistiana world and general authority on just about everything.

'A *real* Aussie, then.'

'Like *you*, you mean.'

'*Exactly*. Another tinny?'

Stewart Carn is as Australian as an import could be – a box at the Opera House, season tickets at the SCG, *Midnight Oil* on the stereo. He is also a man who does exactly what he says – in this case some digging around in Australia about Jem and the young Larry Foley.

'So he was a protégé then?'

'A fan and a fighter.'

'And Jem looked after him. Brought him on. Taught him the "Scientific Way".'

'So Foley could beat Hicken once and for all. That way there'd be an Australian Champion of Australia.'

'Seems only right.'

'Sad, don't you think?'

'Why sad?'

'Because it meant that for the first time your man really knew he was getting old.'

'Fifties is old?'

'How old are you?'

'Same as you.'

'Are we old?'

'Dead right we are.'

Stewart's wife Olivia, who is as graceful as her old man, sets down a platter of seafood. We eat and drink, and afterwards stand out on their balcony, overlooking the sparkling harbour and the wonderful weirdness of the Opera House. Below us, Olivia starts the Mercedes coupé. She waves as she backs out and is gone.

'So,' Stewart says. 'Have you turned into your old man yet?' Which is typical.

'Like *you*, you mean?'

'Oh *sure*.'

'He's rich, you're rich.'

'So?'

'All I'm saying is maybe we all do.'

'So if *your* boy came to *you* and asked for *your* time, would *you* walk away?'

'Maybe I would.'

'You'd stand and watch your boy as he cries and tells you what he's going to do and how he plans to do it, and then just walk away?'

'No-one knows what they'd do.'

From the corner of my eye I see Stewart shaking his head. He always believes the best of people, which is why he's rich and why so many people love him.

'So,' he says after a while, 'this great-great-grandfather of yours. Are you following in his footsteps?'

'I'm here.'

'Have you abandoned your wife and child?'

'Like I say, I'm here.'

'Are you not going back?'

'Is that panic I hear?'

He smiles. 'You're a great dad,' he says, and I have to look away lest he sees my tears.

For Jem it was just like the old days. A travelling boxing booth, a night in one town, a day for travelling, a night in the next. The four of them – Jem, Pooley, Robert Elke and Larry Foley – toured throughout

Victoria and New South Wales, the older man and the younger staging exhibitions and inviting all-comers. Their opponents, for the most part, were farm hands and miners – strong but with no knowledge of ring craft. They'd step up to the cheers of their workmates and families, and for a while they'd appear to be winning, until, unseen by them, a nod would be passed from fighter to trainer, and a 'lucky' blow would be landed that would stand the novice back on his heels, and on the gently disguised road to defeat. It was a game, the outcome of which was already fixed, but none the worse for that. Though beaten, the challenger would have proved his resolve against a man – Jem or Foley – who deserved his admiration. *Next time* he'd say and mean it, though that next time, of course, would never come.

What *did* come one night, in a village way out in the bush, was an incident that would eventually find its way into newsprint from Sydney to London to New York and Norwich, and by word of mouth thence to the village of Beeston.

———

'So they heard about the Ned Kelly incident?'

'Years later. Jem's mother was dead by then, and most of the people in the village who'd known him were gone. One of the few who was still there, of course, was his father, but probably because he was dead too.'

'Which is a lot of use.'

'Exactly.'

'Did your dad know?' says Stewart. 'Is it in the notebooks?'

Yes, I say.

And so it was.

———

According to the *Notes*, Jem and Foley were midway through an exhibition, preparing to invite those young and eager men in the audience to participate, when a band of rough-looking bushmen pushed their way through the crowd, the leader of whom then demanded a sum of money more than twice the combined contents of the pockets of all those present.

'No,' said Jem, and like a gentlemen he apologized.

'You're *sorry?*' said the leader. He was a tall man with a long bushy beard. 'What use is *sorry?*'

Jem glanced to Robert and Pooley, who'd been out in the audience collecting money in a hat. 'That's more than we have,' he said. At this point the leader – soon known to the world as the outlaw Ned Kelly – pulled out a pistol, which, to the gasps of all around, he held to the temple of a flaxen-haired child.

'You English?' he said.

Jem shook his head.

'Then what?'

He was, he said, a gypsy.

Ned Kelly sneered. Feeling the cool of the barrel against his skin, the boy started crying.

'And *you?*' said Jem.

'What *about* me?'

'What are *you?*'

'Australian.'

'And these people – that boy? What part of the world are you from, boy?'

The boy, still crying, shrugged, not understanding.

'He's Australian,' a voice called out.

'Me too,' called another.

'And me.'

'Me too.'

Ned Kelly looked around, feeling suddenly outnumbered.

'Are you planning to shoot that boy?' said Jem. 'Will you do what the Queen and all her policemen couldn't do?'

Slowly Kelly lowered his pistol. The boy ran into his mother's arms.

—•—

'Did that really happen?'

'Really,' I say.

'He just went away?'

'He just went away.'

'Wow.'

'Of course, he killed three policemen later that day. Which is what got him hanged in the end.'

'So another happy ending then.'

'For the boy, certainly.'

'And for Jem. Mind you, being shot dead by Ned Kelly would have saved what was to come.'

'Which was?'

In that moment, Olivia's car sweeps into the drive. As she steps out of the car and looks up and smiles, I'm reminded of my wedding day on a golf course in New Zealand, and how far away that seems now, and how distant and fragile the promises that were made.

30

FOR YOUNG LARRY Foley the benefits of the touring booth were twofold – he gained experience of which he had little, and made some money of which he none. The money he saved, the experience he stored up while he waited for his chance – a chance which came in the wake of an exhibition fight staged in a Melbourne hall rented by Jem for the purpose.

It was a fight that attracted much attention (claims were made that there were more than five thousand people present), not least from Abe Hicken and his cronies. With Mace having allowed Foley a close-fought victory, people said Hicken should face him and decide things once and for all.

The small town of Moama sits on the north bank of the Murray River, three hours by train from the city of Melbourne. Because boxing for money was still nominally illegal in the state of Victoria, it was here – in a place so out of the way and so difficult to get to at that time – that the greatest fight in Australian history would take place, in order to avoid any chance of disruption. It was a fight – as so many have been – with more than simply the victory or defeat of one man at stake. It seemed to stand for something greater. Just as, fifty years later, Max Schmelling and Joe Louis would clearly represent the ideals of the Nazis pitched against those of the free world, here in this small river town were represented the Old World against the New, the forces of Empire against those of independence.

After the first few exchanges the outcome was never in doubt. Foley, equipped with Jem's knowledge and no little skill of his own, was too much for the faded and counterfeit Abe Hicken, who ended the bout, after close to two hours, unable to see and with a busted lip and nose, and no further claims on the territory. It was a seminal event both in Australian sport and the life of Jem Mace. In that moment the colony had anointed its own man as Champion, and Jem had announced his successor. Neither before nor since had he or would he give another man such attention, nor place such a fortune on the outcome of his industry. He was more of a son to Jem than his sons were. If a man's love for his children can be gauged by his attention to them, then Larry Foley was the only one that mattered.

The others were nothing.

But even then, when Jem left Australia with his pockets full of money, he did so without looking back.

———•———

'Did you speak to her today?'

'I've been on a plane. She can't call me on a plane.'

'Well she called *me*—'

'You're not on a plane now. You're in New Zealand. On the ground.'

'So do you want to know what she said or not?'

'Are you going to tell me?'

She shouts and always did, my mother-in-law, in that way that all deaf people do, as if the rest of us are deaf too, or they'd like us to be. Aside from that, though, she's great and loves her daughter as a mother should – with passion and enough clearsightedness to see that even a daughter who's a mother isn't always right.

'Come and sit down,' she says.

Which is not a good sign. You only have to sit down for bad news – a brain tumour, a motorcycle accident, failure to achieve straight A's.

So I sit down, aware as I'm doing so that I'm sitting in my late father-in-law's chair, from which he could watch the garden and the TV with equal clarity. 'What did she say?' I say.

'She said she's been trying to reach you.'

'I know that. Didn't you say that?'

'She said you weren't there for the service.'

'I know that too. *I* was the one that wasn't there.'

'And that my grandson broke his wrist.'

'You're not telling me what I don't know.'

'Well I didn't know.'

'Well nobody told you.'

She pauses, looks down at her hands, then up. 'Can I ask you something?' she says.

'Is that a question?' I say.

Another pause.

'What is it?' I say, though I know very well what it is.

And then she asks me, and though I think I'm ready for it, clearly I am not. *No of course not*, I want to say. *What kind of a father do you think I am?* But the words don't come. They stop in my throat like they want to choke me. I wait for the consoling hand on my shoulder but it doesn't come, and I'm left to sob without comfort, and soon I'm alone in the darkening house, from which, so many years ago, I and the mother of my son stepped out in the broad Christmas sunshine to be married.

——◆——

Nellie Lee was the wife of a man who claimed to be a professor of music, but was no more a professor of music than he was a faithful husband. She was a beauty with a talent for the piano and a strength of mind that men – particularly men like her husband – found both a challenge and a threat.

She was also – Nellie Lee – standing on the quayside in Wellington, when the *SS Melbourne Star* sidled up to the wharf after a thousand mile journey across the Tasman Sea.

She watched and watched and, though face after face appeared, none of them was his. They smiled and some of them raised their arms in greeting, and mothers and brothers and friends and lovers rushed forward to greet a particular arrival. And then suddenly there were no more, and the gangplank was lifted and returned to its place aboard ship, and Nellie Lee, who'd dreamed as a girl of a kind man and a large and loving family, turned away and was alone on the quayside. And when the place had fallen quiet she was standing there still, looking down into the water, as if somewhere in its depths lay comfort and rest.

That night she stayed in a hostel for abandoned women on the edge of Chinese Bay, and in the morning, carrying all that she had in a single carpet bag, she walked slowly into town not knowing what she planned to do.

The name struck her with the force of a memory from long ago.

Jem Mace – Champion of the World.

She stood and stared at the letters on the board outside the theatre, as if to do so would bring some kind of comfort. She was standing there still when the theatre door opened and a large burly man in a bowler hat stepped out before her, his arms folded tight and his feet set firm on the ground in an attitude of refusal.

'Yes?' he said.

'I was just looking,' said Nellie.

'Looking?' said the man, as if to do so were to commit some outrageous and quite unforgiveable crime.

'I'm sorry,' she said and moved on. The man watched her until she was lost from view.

Two nights later she was sitting in the back of the stalls waiting for the show to begin, when the man in the seat beside her placed his hand with no shame on her leg.

She looked at him sharply. He was smiling, a thin man with stains on his jacket and a frayed collar. She covered his hand with hers. His smile broadened, and he leaned towards her and would have stolen a kiss and more, had the pain in his hand not suddenly been so great that he pulled it away with a howl.

'Jesus Christ!,' he shouted, the blaspheming not stemming the flow of his blood. The woman's nails were red too, and now she was the one who was smiling.

'*And now,*' said a voice from the stage, '*the one and only Champion of the World – Mr Jem "The Gypsy" Mace!*'

She sat forward, her heart thumping, as the man she'd once seen at The Cremourne Pleasure Gardens stepped onto the stage.

'Can I help you?'

She thought, at first, that the tall man who answered her knock at the stage door was him.

'Are you him?' she asked, embarrassed at once by the foolishness of the question.

'That depends,' said the man half smiling. 'If it's me you're looking for.'

But it wasn't – something in his look made her sure of this. 'Well,' she said.

The man stepped back with a shrug. 'Welcome,' he said, indicating the way down a narrow hall, 'to the temporary throne room of the King of the World.'

He was lying on a low bed, one arm across his eyes, his chest bare, his other arm trailing the floor.

'Is he all right?' she said softly. She turned but the other man was gone.

She looked back. The room was sparsely furnished – a rack of clothes, a few bottles on a chipped wooden table, the remains of a meal on a plate half hidden by the bed.

Only after the first of his children with his wife was born would Jem tell her the true story of that night – that the whole thing was a set-up that had worked before and many times since, and with far greater beauties than the one he'd been stupid enough to marry. Such a disclosure was spiteful and, for him a way out, for by then he had tired of her, and had chosen to return to the one whose place she'd taken. No doubt he showed remorse – but this was cheap when set beside the damage he'd done. Perhaps the constant need to secure a possible means of escape from anything and everything was necessary for a man of his background, or perhaps he was just a moral coward – more likely it was a combination of both. Whatever, it didn't make him a nice man – but since when does a nice man become Champion of the World?

———⋅—⋅———

'It's possible. Look at me.'

'You're not Champion of the World.'

My brother-in-law Chris drops down to his haunches and lines up the putt. 'Well,' he says, cocking his head and checking the lie, 'in the recycled box world, you know, I probably am.' He stands up and steps back, grips and re-grips his putter.

'But—'

'Ssh.'

The *clock* of putter on ball and it rolls left then right, slows and, edged to hole, slows some more before it drops over and in.

'You were saying?' he grins.

'I was saying that you can't compare the two.'

'Correct me if I'm wrong, but I think you were saying that nice guys can't ever come first.'

'Not where it matters, no.'

'You mean like family?'

'You know that's not what I mean.'

'So what else is there?'

'*Everything* else.'

'None of which matters when your child calls you Daddy.'

I hear myself scoff.

'Well don't you think? I mean who gives a shit about cardboard boxes or boxing or golf or TV when your child's in trouble?'

He reaches down for his ball and there's something in the way he does it that makes me certain he knows.

'And no,' he says as if he's reading my thoughts, 'I don't believe it either.'

'Either?'

'My mother as you know is deaf. That doesn't mean she can't *see* what's going on.'

'Which *is*?'

'I can't believe you don't know.'

'I don't. So tell me.'

He pockets the ball and leans like a landowner on his putter. 'Two things,' he says. 'Firstly, has it ever occurred to you that this wife of yours – my sister – is worried that this Jem of yours will get under your skin so badly that you'll start to take his way of doing things as a good way?'

'Which is ridiculous.'

'Of course it is. But you know why she's thinking like that?'

I shake my head. No idea.

'Okay. This is the other thing. If she can't tell you because you're not there and she can't get a hold of you, who can she tell?'

'*I* don't know. I suppose it depends what *it* is.'

'Well *think* about it.'

I do. Nothing. 'You?' I say.

He shakes his head.

'Her mother?'

He smiles.

'I don't understand,' I say. 'Will you please just tell me?'

And so he does and, standing on the very spot beneath the very tree, under which he stood years ago, as best man, he puts his arm around me with the strength of a father, and holds me firm, as the thought of the arrival of another new life that will need my protection fills me with fear and the most painful and exquisite joy that I have ever known.

'Will you be all right?' We're sitting in his car on the way to the airport.

'Yes,' I say, 'I'll be fine' and for the first time in ages I know I will.

'And this Mace, what about him?'

'What do you mean?'

'What happened to him? Did he stay here? Are there hundreds of you little Maces running around downtown Auckland?'

A part of me wants to say 'Yes', but of course the answer is 'No'. 'They went home,' I say. 'Him and Nellie and Pooley and Robert. Took the boat back to America, and then back to England.'

'Where he was already married.'

'Where he was already married. Which didn't stop him getting married again.'

'But this other woman – she took him back?'

'She did.'

'And the children?'

'Scattered.'

'It's a way of doing things.'

I watch the car pull away until it is gone. I pick up my bag and head into the terminal. I can't wait to get home and start again.

31

But to leave his New Zealand story there would be both unfair and inaccurate – as it would be to state simply that he travelled the country giving talks and exhibitions, in the process of which he made a great deal of money and lost a great deal too. It has been my observation that the Land of the Long White Cloud is and was then a land obsessed with money and particularly with losing it. *If it moves take a bet on it. If it doesn't, put money on how long it will be before it does.*

But for Jem it wasn't just money in and money out. There were women – Nellie and many others – and the whole desperate cycle of self-hatred and revenge – on his poverty, on his ignorance, on his lack of what he thought of erroneously as class. He was determined to earn more than others, and spend more, and sleep with more women – more wives, be they his own or others' – and leave nothing behind him that anyone could claim had been his and was now theirs.

Except of course his children, who were always his, and his belts and the accidental influence he had had on countless lives.

As a younger man I travelled widely across New Zealand (it being so far away and so empty that it was for the most part unreachable by phone), unaware that my great-great-grandfather, about whom I knew nothing, had spent any time there. I didn't know, for example, that he'd taken top billing in a theatre in Wellington or spent a month on the South Island, in what is now a scout hut in the small coastal town of Timaru. When entirely alone I laid myself down in that faraway place, and looked up at the white painted rafters and listened to the pounding of the sea not four hundred yards away. I'd no idea that a hundred years before in that very town, *in that very hall*, Jem Mace had set up a boxing school – The Mace Academy – from which would emerge some of the finest southern hemisphere boxers the world has ever known. All of which he did for nothing – except for whatever pleasure and satisfaction it gave him.

That my father mentioned nothing of this in the *Notes* neither surprises nor disappoints me. He was always one for the drama of bad news.

One thing – person – he *did* mention was Herbert Slade.

———•———

A native of Timaru and half-Maori, Slade was, in appearance, a dark and fearsome man, although his nature was anything but. He was, in fact, a quiet and rather timid man, but it was Jem's view that this could be hidden and nobody need know. Not that he really need have worried for, as soon as 'The Maori Terror' took to the ring, he became a different man – as fearsome in attitude as he was in appearance. When he fought he fought with astonishing brutality and, though sometimes beaten by cleverer men, there was always a return and almost always for Slade – under Jem's tutelage – revenge. In a year he fought nearly sixty bouts and was soon regarded as New Zealand's own Champion.

For Jem, who had his mark on a contract drawn up in Dunedin, this meant a further income and so greater opportunities to add to his losses. The modest property he'd gathered in America was already gone, and much of what he earned he owed to the kinds of people who didn't take well to late payment. He was trapped in a cycle of debt and repayment, and when the latter was impossible he and his band had to keep on the move. When creditors forced the Timaru school to close, they headed north again, and again traded well on the fame of Mace and Slade. Jem gave lavish dinners – often spending the money before it was made – and would have continued to do so, had it not been for the arrival at his shoulder on one such occasion, of a waiter with a silver tray, upon which sat a Western Union cable.

He excused himself and left the table.

'It'll be Her Majesty,' said Pooley, a little too loudly. He raised another glass and downed it.

Across the table, Robert Elke looked ashen.

'What's the matter?' said Pooley, his words starting to slur.

Robert Elke shook his head. The pain in his side he'd been hiding was, at that moment, the worst it had ever been. But he raised a smile and a glass. 'To Her Majesty,' he said. 'May the sword that she lowers on Jem's shoulder be flat side down.' He winced unnoticed.

'Do you think that's it?' said a lady from Taupo.

'*Could* it be?' whispered another. Shoulders were shrugged and plans discretely made (though never of course revealed) to treat the upstart Gypsy better in the future, lest what seemed such an unlikely outcome turned out to be true.

When Jem returned, amid a sense of general excitement, he took his seat beside Nellie, squeezed her hand and resumed eating his dinner.

'Is everything as it should be?' said the lady from Taupo.

Jem nodded without looking up, and soon, reluctantly, the babble of inconsequential talk returned.

When they boarded the ship that would take them back to California it was hard for Jem *not* to think of himself retracing his steps again along a route that once had promised so much, but that now found him famous but so much older. His body ached in the mornings and at night, and his spirit, once incapable of even considering defeat, was now – in his worst moments –no longer that of a bluff and confident fighter, but that of an old man, who longs only for the comforting warmth of family and home.

But where – in these darkest of moments, as the steamer pitched and rolled on the darkness of the sea – would he find such comfort? Where would he find such a home? And how could he rebuild a family that had never been a family in the first place?

There was a bleakness as he stood at the railings and watched the lights of San Francisco edge ever nearer. The wind off the sea was cold, the salt bitter like blood on his lips. He turned away, and would have made his way back to Nellie and their cabin, had he not found her standing there before him huddled up against the cold and a smile of great warmth on her face – like the smile of a mother for her wayward, but favourite, son.

'What is it?' he said.

'You,' she said.

'What about me?'

She paused. 'Can I ask you something?'

He shrugged and looked away out to sea.

'And you must promise to tell me the truth.'

Another shrug.

'Are you happy?'

He turned, frowning, as if the word were perfectly unfamiliar to him.

'Because if you're not...' Her voice trailed off.

'You remember that cable?' he said.

'Cable?'

'That came at dinner. The one I said was from the shipping line.'

Now she was frowning.

'Well it wasn't from the shipping line. It was from Hannah. It was to say that Benny slipped on the ice on the lake at home.'

Nellie made no sound. *It was from Hannah.*

'Anyway he went through—'

'Oh Lord,' she whispered.

'And they tried to get him out, but it was hard, and when they did he was dead.'

—◆—

And when they did he was dead.

Reading this now, I can't help but wonder what my father was thinking when he wrote it. In the *Notes* it seems too easy – the whole scene on the ship way too sentimental. But maybe that's just me. It *happened* and it happened like *that* – and why should it *not*? Maybe my own journey home would be better for a little more feeling, although I have the feeling that, were I to start letting everything out, I just might not be able to stop. And so I shall sit here and drink this Bloody Mary and continue reading the *Notes*, in the absence right now of a life of my own.

32

WITH THE DEATH of Robert Elke, Jem lost the one person in his life who was with him neither through the duty of blood nor the binding grip of avarice. He was there simply through friendship and because he could see something in Jem – a vulnerability, perhaps, or a common need for a father – something that, even now, is sometimes hard to see. His death in far-off Toronto, where he'd gone to visit a relative, heralded the end of something, the significance of which was masked at the time by other events, and would only later be truly felt. At the time, in the weeks building up to Herbert Slade's fight at Madison Square Garden with the fearsome terror that was John L. Sullivan, Jem was troubled more by financial loss than human. Even the death of his son appeared to be a step down in the hierachy of distress, the more immediate worry being his ability to keep *himself* alive.

All of which was made worse for Jem by the knowledge that Herbert Slade was a dud and would never – contrary to what he'd once believed – amount to anything lasting in the fight game. He was strong, certainly, and was willing to learn, but he was not blessed with the capacity to do so. Sullivan, on the other hand – *The Boston Strongboy* – had both strength and a technical ability matched by few. Money placed against him was surely, almost all agreed, money lost.

Almost but not all. There were those who reckoned that a man such as Mace would not settle his reputation on the shoulders of someone likely to lose it. There had to be more to him – this *Terror of the South Seas* – than his manager was showing. More and more came to believe that it was a bluff as the days went by, and soon the betting wasn't all on John Sullivan. Soon Jem, the dark horse, came to dominate the minds, particularly of those small investors who wagered money they could scarcely afford. Slade – like his manager before him – became a big man that a little man could trust in to double his money and save him from the wrath of his landlord.

'It was you that yelled?'

'Yes, sir, it was me.'

In June 1972, around a hundred years after the Slade-Sullivan fight, Madison Square Garden was the venue for Elvis Presley's only ever concert in the City of New York. During that show, midway through the Civil War song, *An American Trilogy*, a southern voice cried out, in a spooky reproduction of the old rebel yell that made both the record and the six o'clock news.

'Had you planned it?'

Vern Chamberlain rocks back in a laugh. 'Planned it? No, sir.' Vern's a big man, and his movments seem to rock the whole row of plastic seats. 'What I'd *planned* you don't want to know, except it had to do with a girl from New Jersey, who worked in my dad's office. *She's* what got me there that night. *I* didn't even *like* Elvis...'

Way below us on the ice, Sean Avery of the New York Rangers is warming up in preparation for that morning's training session.

'And now you work here,' I say.

'Yes, sir, I do.'

'So no more yelling?'

'I try to keep it down to a minimum.'

Down below us Sean Avery throws his stick across the ice in a temper and kicks the low wall.

'Is he all right?'

'He's okay. He's Canadian. What was I saying?'

'About that night.'

'Oh sure. Look, you have to remember I was a young man then, and a southern boy from Mississippi—'

'Just like Elvis. And you've got the same name as his dad.'

'Exactly. And that night, well I was kind of *worked up*, if you know what I mean. And when I heard that song, well it just all came out. Oh, and my mama had just gone into a home, and it looked like she was gonna die.'

CHAPTER THIRTY-TWO

'What happened?'

'She died.'

'I'm sorry.'

'Why? *You* didn't do it.'

On the ice, Alexei Cherepanov is raising and lowering his stick, then twisting this way and that. I feel Vern's eyes upon me.

'*You* ever lost anybody?' he says.

I lie and say *No*.

'Except your dad?'

'How did you know?'

'The way you talk about your boy. Like he's the only way to make things better.'

We sit for a while looking down at the ice. It seems to me that sometimes the deepest secrets a man holds can be read by observing the lines on his face and are only as secret as the onlooker's wish to know them and to either understand or ridicule.

'What are you thinking?' he says after a while.

'I was thinking about Jem. Being here. And how he knew he was finished and that soon all he'd gathered around him would be taken away.'

'There's his memory. There's right now. There's you and me talking about him. Doesn't that mean anything?'

'That's not life. That's history.'

'History is life.'

'History is life that's gone.'

'You mean it's the afterlife?'

I say I don't know, and truly I don't. Sometimes I don't seem to know anything. Sometimes everything just seems like so many words.

A call from the ice.

Vern raises his arm in a wave. 'Jesus,' he says, 'you should see that man's slapshot.' Then he slips me a look that lets me know I'm not alone.

The fight, when it came to it, was exactly what Jem had feared it would be – brains and brawn against brawn, with the former inevitable victors over the latter. Not that Slade didn't do all he could, it's just that all he could do wasn't enough. He threw his punches as Jem had taught him, but seemed to have forgotten the lessons that had to do with defence. He stepped forward in the first round, when he should have stood his ground, and got whacked in the throat for his trouble. He stumbled back until the ropes stopped him and he'd nowhere else to go, and then Sullivan – grinning, cocky Irishman that he was – was upon him, pounding his head until his fists and Slade's face were a bloody mess, and only the mercy of the bell stopped the fight turning into murder.

The second was no better, despite Slade's distant memory of Jem's instruction, for though he tried to step this way and that in an attempt at evasion, his feet were so slow and movement so ponderous that Sullivan could pick him off at will. Which he did. He slammed him with a right and broke his nose and closed the New Zealander's eyes, as surely as if he'd been singing him a lullaby. Blind and stumbling, Slade struck out, swinging but finding nothing, then again, and again, until something seemed to catch his foot and trip him, and the ground seemed to rise up before him, and everything was skewed and on its side, and his body hit the ground like that of a slaughterhouse cow, and at once began discharging blood, sweat and shit, but he didn't care, he was way, way past caring, and all he wanted was to lie there in the warm until his Daddy would come by and rouse him for the day's work—

'Hey, Mace...'

and he and his brothers – all talk and elbows and dreams for the future – would climb into the boat and set out upon the beautiful clear waters of the bay.

'What do you want?' said Pooley.

'I want you to tell him he's finished here. I want you to tell him if he ever comes back he's a dead man.'

Pooley turned away. He looked for Jem in the vicious heaving crowd but found only Robert. He fought his way towards him and placed a hand on his shoulder.

'Hey...'

The man turned. It wasn't him. How could it be? *He* was dead.

Pooley dropped his hand. For a moment, looking into the stranger's bitter face, he felt such a deep longing for the way things had once been, that his breath was hard to gather. As he stood there and saw, in his mind's eye, the two of them up high once again in the old Cutter barn, he knew that promise was richer than reward, except for death, which was both promise *and* reward.

———•———

'So has it helped?'
  'Being here?'
'If you like.'
  'Of course.'
'But I guess it's time to go home, huh?'
  'Somebody else told me that.'
'Well then it must be right.'
  'Right.'
We shake hands.
  'By the way,' he says. 'This Robert. What happened to him?'
'Like I say, he died. Cancer or something like that.'
  'You don't know?'
'I don't know. Nobody knows. It doesn't matter.'
  'Except to him.'
'Well not any more.'
  'You mean you *don't* believe in reincarnation?'
'You mean like he's come back as a goat or something?'
  'A goat?'
'It was just an example.'
  'So where's he buried?'
'Toronto. He had family or something.'
  'Are you going?'
'To Toronto? Why?'
  'See the man's grave.'
I shake my head. 'I've had enough. I want to go home.'
  'Then go.'
And so I did. After so many months away I caught the next plane home.

———•———

When the boat docked in Liverpool, Jem, Pooley and Nellie made their way quietly down the rear walkway and onto a quayside bustling with people, none of whom, this time was here for them. No longer, it seemed, was anyone concerned that the man still nominally Champion of the World had come home. This time there were no banners, and no man from *The Times* there to catch all the gossip and print it as news.

Instead they slipped quietly away, and began life in Nellie's modest family home on the other side of Stanley Park from the home of Liverpool Football Club. Although he'd managed to squander most of his money, Jem still had a small but regular income from an Australian goldmine he'd been persuaded to invest in, along with occasional speaking engagements or requests for autographs, for which he would charge a nominal sum.

To those who knew his history, he was a curiosity, and some pointed him out to others in the street. He would smile, seeming not to mind such a come-down. Indeed, to Nellie, and to others, he claimed to be happy and glad at last to be able to rest.

Not that life in Queen's Road was exactly restful. Even with Pooley having returned to London, the house was seldom quiet, and never a place where a man could retire. Besides Nellie and Jem, there was Nellie's stepson, John, her sister, Annie, and her two children, and soon another child called Ellen, who was Jem's. Of these, ten-year-old John was Jem's favourite, being a bright boy whose talents lay in music. He would play the family piano on Sunday afternoons, and Jem would accompany him on his fiddle. The neighbours would call in, and friends too, and soon the whole house would be filled with singing and laughter and all that a family man would recognize as home.

Which was the problem. The permanence that home implied was anathema to a man with Jem's heritage. He craved it so but dreaded it more. He dreaded Monday mornings that slid without incident into Monday afternoons, and he hated the way that, after a while, no-one bothered to point at him and whisper. He hated the fact that, when the fools at The Crown had had too much and got lairy, they were no longer cowed by the threat of his arrival and the power of his fists. He had settled down but couldn't settle. He had to risk something to prove his existence. He had to gamble and lose what little he had left.

This he did in stages and courtesy of the racetrack. Almost every horse he backed proved to be a three-legged nag, and in defeat each took with it a further portion of the little that remained. And then there was the Grand National, Aintree's annual losers' bonanza, and Jem didn't disappoint. Here he lost most but not all. There was still enough to take him on a quick jaunt to Paris, where something of his famous name remained. Here he refereed a fight, and spent the next day at the track and that night in the bed of a whore. Not content with shedding all he'd worked for and been given, he was seemingly determined to lose Nellie and the children as well.

In this he nearly succeeded.

But not quite, for Nellie Lee was tougher than Jem, in the only ways that matter. She refused to be cast aside and, when Jem told her he'd a chance of buying into a boxing school in London, she packed up his things and hers and those of the children, and down they went. Except this time she was in charge. Things would be bought only when they could be paid for, and not a penny would be wasted on anything that carried odds.

And she nearly succeeded.

But not quite, for though she was strong, she wasn't devious enough, and Jem was a master of deception. He would feint and parry her every enquiry and make a sport of his and their descent. And there was Hannah, still living in the East End where he'd left her, though she, like he, had bigamously married. He taunted Nellie with her, and, afraid of the visible onset of old age, he dyed his hair black, until a once graceful man became a figure of fun.

Of course the Boxing School failed and took with it any possible income and almost all of the money that remained, and they were forced again and again to move to new and always cheaper lodgings. Eventually they had no choice but to drag themselves back up to Liverpool, and to the house they'd left empty in Queen's Road. From here, after a month of penitent living, his old ways took hold of him again. He would hang around the theatres and talk with the show-folk – in particular the actresses, to most of whom he was unknown but had, despite his age and the colour of his hair, some remnants of what had once made him such a ladies' man. They laughed at his jokes and his stories of his travels, and some slept with him out of boredom or for money. Sometimes, on a whim, he'd go to London and meet up with some old crony from his ring days.

They'd get drunk and talk about old times and he'd somehow make the long journey home.

It was on one such journey that Jem met a man whose connections would provide him with a brief and unexpected season of warmth before the final winter and his fall.

33

HUGH CECIL LOWTHER had been an acrobat in Switzerland, a cowboy in New Mexico and many other things, including an Arctic explorer, when his father passed away and he became, at the age of twenty-nine, the 5th Earl of Lonsdale.

A practical joker who had once, for a dare, tried to hold up a stagecoach on the outskirts of Denver with nothing but a smile and a rolled-up copy of the *Rocky Mountain News*, he struggled at first with the burden of the title, but after a while he began to find it quite to his liking. A devotee of yellow, he decreed that the staff at Lowther Castle in Cumbria should all be suited out in that colour, and also that the collection of early motor cars he'd so painstakingly amassed should be painted likewise. He was gloriously mad with a solid streak of sense running through him. He was a gentleman philanthropist who took the view that all men were equal but only some of them were lucky. He was known as The Yellow Earl, and sometimes The Lucky Earl, both of which appellations were accurate until a certain morning one March, when his bride, Lady Grace Gordon, fell from her horse whilst out riding and the doctors were called to her bedside.

That she lived but would never bear a child doomed the Lonsdale name to extinction and their marriage to a long and sterile death. The Earl had his affairs (once memorably with the actress Lily Langtry, herself the mistress of the Prince of Wales), while his wife had her good causes. They were the look-outs, last to leave a slowly-sinking ship, gatekeepers still protecting a once fertile but now barren estate. And everything around them was painted the colour of sunshine, as if in mockery.

'Cigar?'

Jem opened the eyes that drink and exhaustion had closed. 'Where are we?' he asked. 'And who are you?'

The thin man in the fine suit glanced out of the train window at the fields passing by. 'Perhaps Northampton,' he said with distaste. Again he proffered the cigar. 'Would you care for one?' he said.

Jem pushed himself up. What had once been a fine athletic body was now that of a foolish old drunk. He took the cigar. The thin man lit it then one for himself. 'By the way,' he said, 'the Earl sends his condolences.'

Jem removed the cigar. 'What?'

'On the death of your cousin.'

'How did you know that? Who *are* you?'

'The Earl has a great interest in the art of boxing and has acquaintances in the United States, who keep him informed of, shall we say, *developments*.'

'That's great. But what has that got to do with me?'

'You are the Champion.'

'So?'

'*So*, the Earl feels that such an accomplishment should not be forgotten.'

'Well tell him thanks. Is that it?'

'And that he'd very much like to make your acquaintance.'

Jem lowered his cigar and squinted through the smoke.

'Would that be possible?' the man asked.

'Why?'

'If you'd like we could go at once.'

'Go where?'

'The Earl has a house.'

'Good for him.'

'In Cumbria.'

'Cumbria?'

'So will you come?'

'What does he want?'

'That's not for me to say.'

'Then the answer's no.'

'The Earl will be very disappointed.' The thin man with the fine suit stood up.

'Where are you going?'

'If you should change your mind you will find me in the dining car. Goodbye.' He turned and made his way down the carriage.

CHAPTER THIRTY-THREE

The yellow suit was preposterous as was the notion of his being there at all. Jem was a much married man and a father many times over, and had fought for and won the Championship of the World. And now look at him. An old man and an employee of an Earl living in a castle on the edge of a lake.

'Is the place to your taste?'

'It's not what I'm used to.'

'Most people call me sir.'

'It's not what I'm used to, *sir*.'

'But they're fools. *You* can call me Cecil. If you choose.'

They were standing, the Earl and the Champion, in a high-ceilinged wood-panelled room, whose windows overlooked the vast estate. Both men were stripped to the waist, the older of the two a little heavier than he'd once been and considerably less toned. Both had been sweating hard, lifting weights.

'So tell me what do think about my plan?' asked the Earl.

'Sir?'

'*Please*.'

'Cecil.'

'That's better. So do you think Her Majesty would approve?'

'I don't know. How would I know?'

The Earl wiped his face with a towel. When he lowered it his hair was everywhere, and his face flushed making him look like a little boy. 'Was she terribly sad?' he said.

Jem said that she'd seemed so, though it was difficult now precisely to remember the details of that long-ago afternoon.

'Did you know she's dying?'

Windsor. The Great Room. Her pale face and hands. It all seemed so distant now.

'Whether she'll see the new century nobody knows.'

'She's strong.'

'It'll be the century of the motor-car. And man will fly. You'll see.'

Jem was looking out at the rolling lawns and the woodland beyond, which descended in a slow and gentle arc to the lake. A figure was sitting, knees gathered, far off in the shade of an oak tree.

'What is it?'

'Someone sitting. A girl. Beneath that tree. There.'

The Earl crossed to the window.

'Do you see her?'

He shook his head. Jem stood beside him. The girl, if she'd ever been there, was gone.

'It must be my eyes,' said Jem.

The Earl smiled. 'Too many knocks to the head, eh? Or perhaps too many wives.'

Jem turned away from the window. For a moment he tried to picture Nellie's face but could see only Hannah's. In his mind's eye she was lying on her sickbed again, the froth in her lungs bubbling every time she tried to breathe. Then she was cold and pale in death and he was at her side, and then Nellie's warm hands were upon him again, and again she forgave him, but her forgiveness was again just a broken busted currency to be squandered on a girl young enough to be his daughter.

'I was wondering—' said the Earl.

Jem looked up.

'—who'll carry your legacy. If there'll be fighters in your family when you're gone.'

'With children you don't know.'

'But you know your children.'

It was something they'd not talked about – children, having them but not knowing them, not being able to have them and knowing all that your ancestors have painstakingly gathered will be scattered again and lost.

'I do,' said Jem, though both men knew it was a lie.

'That's good. A man should know his children. And save them if he can.'

Jem said nothing. He was old and he knew such a thing was beyond him. He didn't care enough, and never had, and now he was just tired.

The Earl pulled his silk shirt over his head. 'Until tomorrow then,' he said.

'Until tomorrow then,' said Jem, and when he was alone and the blue linen shadows were drawing slow across the lawn, he looked again for the girl by the oak tree.

34

ONCE A MONTH we take our son to Brighton in the car and sit on the pebbles and watch the sea. In the Winter we take Annie the dog too. She runs along the water's edge barking at the pier and is surprised every time by the wetness of the water. Sometimes in summer, the boy and I take a stroll through the Lanes while his mother sunbathes. Often we end up outside a shabby, white, terraced house, the windows of which have lately been covered with newspaper – whether because of refurbishment or in the absence of curtains I don't know. We don't say much as we stand there. Sometimes he holds my hand, sometimes not.

It was here that Jem Mace had his last proper home. It was here that he lived with Alice, an actress half his age, whom he'd watched from the stalls of the Prince of Wales Theatre in London. Because of his history she had thought him wealthy (she believed the shabbiness of his outfit to be mere affectation), and though she soon discovered otherwise she had already fallen in love with him – or at least felt sufficient pity for him to confuse it with love.

'What do you want?'
    Alone this time, having left the boy with his mother, I have decided to knock on the door.
    'A family member,' I say, 'used to live here. I was wondering—'
    The door slams, the knocker rising and falling. I try again.
    'I *said* go away.'
    This time the door opens only a crack.
    'You didn't actually,' I say.
    'Whatever.'
    'I don't want anything.'

'Then go away.'
'Except to see.'
'See what.'
'Where he lived before he died.'
'Who?'
I explain. For some reason it does the trick. I am ushered inside.

———•———

They had a child called as Lillian, and it was to this terrible place
– it was as run-down then as it is today – that the three of them
descended, when the rent went unpaid on a larger and cleaner place
in Queen's Road. Jem worked as a violinist, sometimes in one of the
theatres and sometimes in the arcade. He drew pitying glances from
the few who knew his history, and vicious taunts from those who
knew of his relationship with Alice. These he endured, for her sake
alone. He had to play, for if he didn't, the three of them didn't eat.
Soon, however, the legacy of his fighting denied him even this means
of a living, as his fingers began stiffening with arthritis. And thus was
his financial ruin complete.

———•———

'What are you looking for?'
It's hard to find the *then* in the *now* – to see and share a vigil with
the ghosts of those departed.
'I don't know.'
'Do you want a cup of tea?'
We sit on the floor amid the last of Nina's things. She's moving
away from Brighton to live with her parents in Bexhill. Only twenty-
four years old, she is already a widow, her husband having been
blown to bits by an IED in Afghanistan.
'Sugar?'
She has yet to collect the possessions he left behind him.
'I don't know what I was expecting,' I say when she returns.
'*Something*. But there's nothing. I feel nothing. And he suffered so
here. Real poverty. Real pain. You'd think *something* would be left
of it.'

CHAPTER THIRTY-FOUR

And then it occurs to me – the crassness of what I've just said.

'Don't worry,' she says. 'Most people don't know what to say around me, so they end up saying nothing. Just smiling and touching. I hate it.'

Smiling and touching.

'Can I ask you something?' I say.

'If you want.'

'It's not a question with an answer.'

'Good. That's the best kind.'

'If someone close to you – I mean really close, a parent say – walked away from you when you really needed them, would you ever forgive them?'

'That depends.'

'On what?'

'On whether or not I had a child, or would ever have a child.'

'Why?'

'Because if I *did*, or was going to, I'd want to know that I'd be forgiven when I walked away.'

'Are you saying it's inevitable?'

'The walking or the forgiving?'

'Either. Both.'

'Are you saying that it *isn't*?'

'I don't know.'

'Why take the chance?'

'Then you would. Forgive.'

'I hope so.'

'Have you?'

'Not yet.'

'Will you?'

'One day.'

She is watching from the window as I close the gate behind me. I wave and she smiles, and I watch her turn away. I think of the day when she finally collects her dead husband's things and how strong the impulse will be just to lay herself down in the safe embrace of mourning and let the cool tide overtake her and just carry her away.

But then I feel certain that impulse will pass and she'll push herself up, and in time be a mother to children who will forgive and be forgiven, and they'll pass in the street one day, her child and mine, unaware of the pain of their pasts.

'So did you find what you were looking for?'

    'There's a story I want to tell you about Jem.'

    'Now?'

    'Let me read it to you.'

    So, with the boy tossing stones into the sea and delighting in their sound, I fetch out the *Notes* for just about the last time.

    'Is it sad?' she says.

    'Yes.'

    'Is it the end?'

    'Not quite. But close.'

    She lays back on the pebbles and closes her eyes, and I know in that moment that something at last is lifting from me. As I turn the pages I think of my father and how warm his feet were to stand upon on those cold winter nights, and how strong his arms were, wrapped around me in a way that made me feel he might never let me go.

PART FOUR

Never Walk Alone

35

THE QUEEN WAS dead and everything he'd ever known was changing. Motor-cars and man's first attempts at powered flight were both connecting the world and threatening to shrink it, and the phonograph, with its crackling disembodied voices, became, and remained, the new century's soundtrack. In Switzerland Albert Einstein had rewritten Galileo, while in America Israel Isidore Baline had earned thirty-seven cents for his first ever song, and promptly changed his name to the snappier Irving Berlin.

'James Mace?'

She opened the door just enough to see.

'We have a warrant.'

'Good for you.'

She tried to close it, but a heavy boot prevented her. 'We don't want any trouble,' said its owner, nor did he, for he was weary of his work and longed instead to buy a small boat and offer tours around the new Palace Pier. 'I must discharge my duty and no more.'

Alice Mace dropped her hand and stepped back. The struggle that had, for a long while, seemed noble, these days just seemed pointless. These days she just thought, *Let them take what they want, and maybe when they're done they'll just leave us alone.*

'Is he here – your husband?'

But this they never seemed to do.

She led the two men to the back room. Here a small child and a baby were sleeping in a cot, the baby wrapped up in the child's slender arms. What the two men had come for was on a table by the wall.

'He's out,' she said, then as an afterthought added, 'It's good news.'

The two men glanced at each other with a look Alice recognized. She had seen it so often in the streets of the town and on the Front that it no longer touched her.

'There,' she said indicating the table.

The two men worked quickly but with surprising care. Whether this was through courtesy Alice doubted. More likely it was in order to protect, and so not devalue for resale, the precious belts and cups that had taken Jem most of a lifetime to collect, but which now, with the click of a door and the fading sound of footsteps, were gone.

She sat in the front room so as not to wake the children. She felt almost relieved that the day was nearly over. She waited for her husband to return.

It's good news.

The offer had come quite out of the blue. Six hundred dollars a week for ten weeks' worth of exhibitions in America, and all he had to do was send a photo. For this she'd trimmed his hair and dyed it jet black and, though deep into his seventies, he'd started lifting weights again to show them that, though he was old, he had lost nothing of his young man's physique. He'd walk briskly along the front every morning and to the end of the pier and back, and feel a lightness in his mood he'd not felt for many years.

This was it, he'd tell himself, and they'd started making plans. The boys would attend school and become real Americans, and one day perhaps they'd own houses with porches and raise children of their own, who knew nothing of poverty and hunger.

She woke at the sound of the door.

And all it would take was a single photograph to make it happen.

'Jem?'

She didn't need to see him, or to hear him, to know. That he ventured into the house no further than the hall told her, leaving no room for doubt, that the dye and the exercise had all been for nothing, and that the cable he'd so hurried from the house and through the streets to receive, contained not the words she'd prayed for but those she'd expected and known would come all along.

She heard the door open again and close. She found the cable in the hall.

We regret to inform you...

She opened the door and stepped onto the street. At first she couldn't see him but then there he was, or maybe it was someone else, just some old man on the corner looking up at the gulls and the pale sky beyond, ludicrous with his dark hair, all nobility gone, and just something of the little lost boy remaining.

—————

There is very little of the *Notes* left. A few pages detailing the final moments of the fall is all. And yet there is something in this approaching end that is also exhilarating – much as returning home after a long journey is often both sweet and bitter in equal measure.

'Will that be it? Will it be over then?'

I write these lines in the upstairs back bedroom of a small terraced house not far from Stanley Park in Liverpool. From the window before me I can see a part of what I believe to be the Liver Building and beyond that the grey River Mersey, and beyond *that* Birkenhead. It was here to this house that Jem and Alice fled, when nothing was left for them in Brighton; and it was from here, one Sunday afternoon, that Jem left, on what would become his final journey.

It was only a short walk to the Empire Theatre and then a climb of sixty-eight stairs to the cheapest seats.

Although the view was restricted and his eyesight failing, Jem could still see clearly enough the fake moustache on the face of *Mr Mystery the Magician*, and the décolletage displayed with some gusto by the girls in the chorus. One of these girls in particular took Jem's eye. She was small and slim and dark, and reminded him when she smiled of Adah Mencken.

At the end of the show, and when the theatre had cleared, he made his way down the stairs and around the back to the stage door. Here, straightening himself up so as to banish the years, he knocked on the door.

The sound of footsteps, a lock turning.

'Yes?' said a voice to which there was no reply.

The doorman, who had once been a boxer himself, looked down. There before him on the cobbles, having fallen for the last time, his eyes open as if he were studying the sky for a change in the weather, lay the body of the Champion of the Whole Wide World, finally at rest.

———•—•———

'There's just one more thing to do.'

'And then you'll be home?'

'And then I'll be home. I promise.'

I set down the phone. *One more thing*. In fact it occurs to me there are two. I close the door behind me, make my way down the stairs and leave the house. It's cold in the street and even colder ten minutes later, as I stand beside a marker in Anfield Cemetery.

'This wasn't always here you know.'

'The headstone?'

Mr Forrester, one of the gardeners, shakes his head. 'For years,' he says, 'there was nothing to tell it from the others. Just a number. People would come and just walk past, not knowing who was here.'

'Do you think they would have cared?'

'Some people did. Enough anyway to pay for this.'

We stand for a while in contemplation of the grave. The church in Beeston and the start of my search seem both a mile and a thousand miles away.

'Ten minutes and we're closing.'

I thank the man and shake his hand. I stand a while longer beneath the darkening skies then turn away myself, my journey and his finally over. It's time to go home.

———•—•———

EPILOGUE

Notes for a Life

I AM PERSUADED by a friend of mine to include the following – the last, that is, of my father's *Notes*. This final installment may (as has been suggested) add something to what has gone before in the way of explanation. Consequently, I shall quote it here without comment or addition.

> *My Dear Son,*
> *The fact that you are reading these words means that I am no longer here to engage in any disputes with regard to their truthfulness or otherwise. Consequently, I can at last say my piece without the interruption of argument.*
>
> *Firstly, on the subject of the Notes themselves, it would be poetic of me to claim that I am grateful for the chance to pass them on to you so that you may write the book that I had always intended to write but never seemed to get to. The truth is, however, simply that I have nothing else to leave you, and that to leave you with nothing would, I believe, be unseemly for a man of my reputation and surely meet with your mother's disapproval.*
>
> *Secondly, the question of that afternoon in my flat which marked the beginning of what you would no doubt describe as our 'estrangement'. It would be useless, I know, for me to try to persuade you now that what you saw as my abandoning you at your most vulnerable time (and so, consequently, being responsible for the near-fatal actions you subsequently chose to take) was simply my need to take a 'breather' – to, as you might say, 'get my head around' what you were telling me about certain events in the past and your immediate intentions.*
>
> *I will admit that my absence in what I see now was a critical moment was an error, and one for which I shall always*

reproach myself. Don't forget, however, that as soon as the kettle had boiled and the tea had been made, I did return – though, as you know only too well, too late. But perhaps all of this matters little now, as the natural order of generations will have been restored with my death.

Thirdly, if anything good can come of the 'situation' that seems to have existed for so long, let it be this. Let what happened on that day be an example – a warning from history, if you like. Should it ever happen that you are that old man in the flat and that your son is the young man on the sofa (all this may well happen, regardless of how unlikely it might seem to you today), allow the confusion to whirl inside your head and don't waste the time in trying to understand it. Perhaps it takes an old man to know that understanding is overrated – and so are the curative qualities of a well-brewed cup of tea. No, if it should come to you to do or to not do what I did, then take the latter course. There is, after all, no misery that absence can cure, no pain that cannot be lessened by the touch of a father's hand.

Which, it seems, is all I have to say.

Except for one thing.

If, on clearing out my things, as I know you and your sister are bound to do, you should come across a small piece of lace wrapped in an envelope and hidden at the bottom of the left-hand desk drawer, take it and, should your boy ever marry, see that he gives it to his bride on the morning of their wedding.

I cannot promise that it will bring him any more luck or happiness than he deserves. I can, however, promise that should all I have believed for so long be proved incorrect and that there is some kind of Heaven, then rest assured that your mother and I will look down upon him and watch over him with all our might, and that I shall do whatever is in my power to stand with him and share whatever pain may assail him, as I failed to do on that long ago afternoon for you, my own brave and most beautiful boy.

Also by Jeremy Poolman:

Fiction

Interesting Facts About the State of Arizona
Audacity's Song
My Kind of America
Skin

Biography

A Wounded Thing Must Hide: In Search of Libbie Custer